BECOMING COMPLETE

BECOMING COMPLETE
Embracing Your Biblical Image

MARION DUCKWORTH

MULTNOMAH · PRESS

Portland, Oregon 97266

Cover design by Al Mendenhall

BECOMING COMPLETE
© 1985 by Multnomah Press
Printed in the United States of America

Library of Congress Cataloging in Publication Data

Duckworth, Marion.
  Becoming complete.

  1. Women—Religious life. 2. Woman (Christian theology)
3. Identification (Religion) 4. Duckworth, Marion.
I. Title.
BV 4527.D83   1985   248.8'43   85-10465
ISBN 0-88070-099-8

85 86 87 88 89 90 − 10 9 8 7 6 5 4 3 2 1

To Grandma and Mama
and all the women who modeled wholeness for me.
God knows who you are.

CONTENTS

TO THE READER

The most desperate struggle of my life has been to satisfy my ache for a personhood in whom I could live at peace. When I was past forty, I finally found her.

I know now with unshakable certainty who I am. And I know my definition is accurate because it's firmly rooted in the Word revealed by God.

The Marion I am today bears little resemblance to the one I used to be. For this I praise God from the insides of my soul and spirit. I am full of joy, and want you to be too. For that reason, I am sharing with you the principles that enabled me to become a whole woman.

Marion Duckworth

STARTING
YOUR
JOURNEY

1. Read this the way you would any other book. Think through the exercises included in each chapter. Or you may prefer to read the book through once, and then go back later to think about them.

2. Use the book as a study guide in your women's group. Read a chapter and do the exercises privately. (There are additional exercises at the end of the book.) Use what you've written as a foundation for group discussion.

3. Keep a spiritual journal as you read. Use the exercises in each chapter as well as those at the end of the book to help you discover how each truth applies to you.

KEEPING A SPIRITUAL JOURNAL

I know from personal experience how valuable journal keeping can be in one's journey from fragmentation to wholeness. Almost ten years ago, I began to write in a green plastic loose-leaf notebook I'd reclaimed from one of my sons at the end of the school year. I've been keeping journals ever since.

As I verbalized my thoughts and feelings on paper, they became more cohesive and concrete. Since then, I've met many women (not writers) for whom a spiritual journal was one of the most important tools in their spiritual maturity. Between the covers, they built a personal body of truth, the way I did. *This is what I believe*—about God, myself, priorities, my relationship to others.

There are no rules for keeping a spiritual journal. Whether you were good in composition in school or can spell well doesn't matter. No one will grade your work. Use any notebook with which you feel comfortable. Most important is to write honestly, putting down what you really think and feel. You are not obligated to write every day, unless you want to.

Write your prayers. Write your insights when you read Scripture and other books. Record thought-provoking experiences as well as your observations. Write down problems and possible solutions. Reminisce. Put down dreams and longings. Draw sketches, write poems or songs if you like. Make lists ("The way I'd like to change"; "Things that make me happy").

Begin with the exercises in this book. It was ones like these that helped me discover my true identity. Use them to stimulate your thoughts.

Keep writing. The Spirit of Understanding will be your teacher, helping you apply eternal principles to your own life. Let him take you on a journey from fragmentation to wholeness.

SEARCHING FOR THE WOMAN WITHIN

Mama wore housedresses to bed. She brought some home from the Brooklyn workshop where they were made and given to the poor. After putting one on, she came into the kitchen for me to see. "They'll make good nightgowns," she shrugged, looking down at it. "I don't have anything to sleep in."

I felt obliged to lie. "It's pretty, Mama." I wished she could become a lady at night wearing a soft, white nightgown with pink and blue embroidery, instead of going to bed in the same kind of clothes she wore to sweep the floor and do the laundry. But she went to bed Mama the housewife and got up Mama the housewife. Sometimes, she did become someone else. I loved the afternoons she was Mama, Friend of the English Lady. She'd recomb her hair, maybe twist it into two buns at the nape of her neck instead of the usual one, and even put on lipstick. The two women sat drinking tea in the English Lady's apartment or ours, talking in whispers, laughing out loud. She was still housewife, though, wearing one of those dresses, and Mama, too, telling me to "go out to play" so I wouldn't hear them talk.

Every other Sunday she became Ingrid's niece. She put on her rust-colored three-piece suit left from the days when she had money in the bank, I put on the gray one she'd made me from material Ingrid had given her, and we'd take the BMT subway to Flatbush. We'd eat chicken or roast beef at the kitchen table with Mama's niece and her husband, the apartment house super, and then go into the living room where I picked out tunes softly on the piano while the adults talked. By five o'clock we were on the BMT heading for home and the nighttime and daytime housedresses.

I knew her as other Mamas, though. The Christian one sat straight and sober in the pew or rocked and read her Bible. When a letter came from Grandpa or one of my aunts or uncles, she became daughter and sister.

"Pop says the pears are good this year," she'd say in the voice she used when she was talking to herself outloud. "Alma's moved. I wonder . . . "

There was a secret Mama, too, Daddy's wife. But he was sick in the hospital and would never get well, so that Mama was hidden inside her head. I loved to get peeks at her, like the times she'd say, "Once when Daddy was well he took me into this expensive shop in New York City and told the clerk to find me a fancy dress and never mind the price."

The sick Mama scared me. "Call the doctor," she'd tell me when she had one of her heart spells. The doctor came and warned, "Two weeks in bed, Mrs. Siegel. No getting up for any reason." For the two weeks she lay helpless and I took care of her. Before school I gave her a basin of water so she could wash, made her breakfast, put a can of soup, a pot, kettle, tea bags, dish, cup, spoons, bedpan, and radio alongside the portable stove. After school I cleared away the dishes, did my homework, and made supper.

From my relationship with Mama, I received my first impressions of woman and of who I was. Besides Mama, there were others who taught me. I was cousin of Janet, Rhoda, Ruth, Madeline, Sidney, Sherwood, Wilfred, Austin, Herbie, Norman (and Billy, too, but he died and I couldn't be his cousin anymore). Then I became someone's real friend. She was Alice, and we played house almost every day, using leaves for dishes and sticks for food.

My world expanded and I expanded my idea of who I was when I went into Mrs. Chapman's first grade and became student, my first real role. I spun fine threads of friendships with second seat fourth row and fifth seat last row.

To daughter, cousin, friend, and student, I added feature writer on the school newspaper and actress in the senior play. Other roles like best softball player I wanted but couldn't achieve because I kept missing the ball with the bat.

The year I was fourteen I was hired to sell penny candy, soda pop, sandwiches, and ice cream in the little store across from the high school. During the hours I worked alone cleaning the pop cooler and stocking the case, I was grown up Marion Siegel working for money just like my Uncle Stanley. As I stood waiting for a six year old to choose how to spend the penny in his fist, I savored the years between us and my right to tell him to "hurry up" when he took too long.

But other Marion Siegels beside clerk kept crowding the tiny store. During lulls in business, I had to be student, too, in order to "get this English composition done for fourth period tomorrow." Evenings when I worked late and Mother came to walk me home, I was daughter as well as clerk and student because I offered Mama a bottle of pop and told her about the day.

Candy store clerk retired at sixteen for waitress. That Marion wore sensible shoes with arch supports and a uniform with a pocket for tips. She lived for a summer and then retired for high school senior. The following June she walked off the auditorium platform, out of student and into career woman.

Mama died and daughter was lowered into the ground with her and covered with earth.

The next several years roles came so fast they left me panting. I became fiancée, then wife, mother of John, then Paul. On a Sunday evening in 1955, I received Jesus Christ as personal Savior and became Christian. After that I was Sunday school teacher, mother of Mark, rural missionary, Bible teacher.

SEARCH FOR A SATISFACTORY SELF

I dashed from accomplishment to accomplishment, role to role, an actress in simultaneously running plays. *This is woman*, I thought when I collapsed between acts to catch my breath.

Woman is not singular. She is plural; the sum of her roles. A row of costumes, each with appropriate props hanging in the closet. For Christian, a Bible, Sunday school quarterly, church directory. For career woman, heels and hairspray and cans of efficiency.

Journal Exercise: Think about the people that helped form your concept of what woman is. Write the impressions they gave you in your journal.

SOCIETY TELLS US WHO WE ARE

Roles and relationships are not the only things that tell a woman who she is to be. Society does, too. From generation to generation and culture to culture, however, its message changes.

In today's western world, ad agency hype describes her as slim, muscle-toned, and assured in her blue wool by day and silver lamé by night. She is efficient and confident, whether making decisions in her skyscraper office or serving chicken to her family.

Endlessly maternal she makes her two scrubbed, freckle-faced children's cuts painless and keeps their diets balanced. She is a grade A housewife with sanitized bathroom bowl and laundry the whitest white and smelling country fresh. Her husband's weekend pal on the ski slopes, she is also his orgasmic lover in the bedroom.

Feminism has had a major influence on society's concepts. "The only way for a woman, as for a man, to find herself, to know herself as a person, is by creative work of her own. There is no other way."[1] They said it everywhere: on Merv and Phil, in the top ten books, in slick newsstand magazine articles.

THE CHURCH SPEAKS, TOO

The church defined woman as well. A few decades ago it said *Home. Wife. Mother. Sunday school teacher.*

Women's missionary society. Adam's rib. The role models it held up were Mary the mother of Jesus and Dorcas who sewed coats for the poor.

Gradually the church modified its message. "Some women *have* to work." Then, "Many women *do* work." And she was given permission, if reluctant and unspoken. Secular and sacred environments sounded less and less dissimilar. Career was seen less as a before-children stint. It was until retirement with maternity leaves of absence.

MODERN WOMAN'S PREDICAMENT

Modern woman charted her course. "I'll finish school, get started in my field, marry, have children." Unconsciously, she acquired a formula for success: education plus career plus Christ plus money plus love/marriage/family equals self-actualization.

The sequence of events may differ from woman to woman, but when she reaches her mid-thirties or so, a woman may feel as though it's time to reevaluate her life. She begins to feel unfulfilled. Fragmented. Not sure who she is because she is trying to be so many things.

She may sense it late in the evening when she's shed her last identity and sits in silence or when her last child goes to school and she experiences what Conway calls "the quiet nest." She may not sense it till her last child walks out for a life of his own and her mother identity seems to walk out with him. She then becomes aware of a vague inner desire for freedom to be the person she wants to be, to be all that she should be as a woman.

Her discontent grows more pronounced, oozing like seepage from the basement. Her boss calls for more coffee, her kids whine for more cookies and she grows angry. "Is this all there is?" she keeps asking herself.

Her Christian self is ashamed and chastises her. She feels guilty, pushes back her anger, and promises herself a long bath behind a locked door.

If she does manage the bath, she feels relieved. Indulged. Relaxed. *I'll do better,* she vows. *Won't let things get to me.*

But things do get to her, and though she soaks for a long time, baths don't penetrate deeply enough. Nothing does for long. Not even the Bible verses she tapes on the dashboard to learn on the way to work or over the sink while she washes the dishes.

She can't talk to her husband about the way she feels, or she doesn't have a husband to talk with. So she reads make-overs in *Woman's Day* and thinks about cutting her hair or changing her make-up . . . maybe having her colors done.

She reads a book or watches a TV documentary about "Women on the Move" and wonders if she's in a rut. A night class? A new job? A hobby? More sleep? Watch what I eat? An evening away from the old routine?

But a day or a week later she faces those moments again when she feels isolated in a crowded world or crushed against the wall by demands.

She's tired: of her job, but she can't quit. Of listening to her parents serve critical clichés with Sunday dinner and of holding in the sharp-edged words she wants to say back. Of sneers or blank looks from her children. Of a house so empty that her own thoughts seem like screams.

She crowds her life to the edges with things to do, people to see, places to be. She joins the choir, is program committee chairperson for Women's Ministries, and counts on Barbara Cartland novels to get her through. And wishes to God that the latest Christian book, the Bible verses, and prayers were enough.

For most women the day does come when their identity as Joe's wife, Mr. Devonshire's secretary, Eve's mother, President of the Guild isn't enough. They feel it when they pick up a magazine but can't concentrate because their mind is too preoccupied with the

21

responsibilities of their roles. *When can I type those reports? What should I buy for Sunday dinner?* "The life of multiplicity . . . it leads not to unification but fragmentation,"[2] Anne Morrow Lindbergh says.

If only I was more than just Mommy and Honey and Get those papers out by five o'clock Mrs. Eubanks. If only there was a woman inside my nightgown every morning who didn't have to do something to be somebody. A woman with her own identity, with an integrated self in which she could live. Who could be depended on to cope with the kids, husband, parents, and nosey neighbors. One who could go from oatmeal to night-night without shattering. A woman who could not be drawn, quartered, sliced up, and given away.

Career has not produced such a woman. Neither has marriage nor children nor learning to weave or paint. Not even the years in a pew (of this she is most ashamed).

Journal Exercise: Write a paragraph describing yourself, but do not mention any of your relationships, roles, and accomplishments. Do not say, "I am Hank's wife, I am Susie's mother, I play the piano for the primary department, I work as a bank teller."

But perhaps you haven't missed your real self yet. Perhaps for now, jobs and family are enough. But eventually, for most of us, it does happen. One woman in her early thirties said, "All I wanted was to make it in my profession. Now, I've finally done it, and I'm happy so long as I'm at work. But success doesn't fill up the rest of my life."

A woman who was searching for a personal identity stretched out her arms at her sides as she talked with me. "All my life I've been giving chunks of myself away. 'Here, want a piece? Go ahead help yourself.' Now, I feel as though there's nothing left."

She dropped her hands at her sides. "The real me simply doesn't exist."

At forty I felt the same way. I seemed only to be the sum of my roles and relationships. Timidly, I began the search, peeking inside my missionary and Mama and wife costumes, like a pubescent looking for breasts. Did such a person exist? Had she been lost on her way through childhood?

I searched others' faces for a reflection of myself. *Have you seen her? Her name is Marion Duckworth.*

1. Betty Friedan, *The Feminine Mystique* (New York: W.W. Norton Co., 1963), p. 344.

2. Anne Morrow Lindbergh, *Gift from the Sea* (New York: Random House 1965), p. 26, 27.

AN
OUT-OF-KILTER
TOWER

I'd been so busy trying to be the person others implied I should be that I never found out who I was. Those times when I was alone and became introspective, I saw so many inadequacies that I felt ashamed. *Is this person who I really am?* Supposing that to be true, I turned away, busying myself by planning dinner for tomorrow or figuring out how to make more closet space.

Often it does seem less painful to wear costumes and pretend no one's home underneath than to own the person we see inside. At midlife, when I lost the missionary role I'd depended most on for identity, I had no alternative but to find out who I really was.

The first thing I had to do was admit that I did have a separate personhood who was me. I had not lost her on my way through childhood. But because she seemed flat, scrawny, underdeveloped and ugly—not the acceptable self I wanted—I had hidden her beneath my costumes like a disfigured child. That way, I could deny she existed at all.

The concept of myself as ugly and unacceptable was one I had been putting together since my earliest days. Like the rest of us, I wasn't born knowing who I am. To find out, I peered inward at the figure inside my human frame called my "self." But the curtains were drawn, the Marion within obscured. I had to count on others to describe her to me.

They obliged. At seven years, I overheard a friend of Mama's talking to her. "Marion's a good kid, but she'll never be the woman you are." *Never as good as Mama.*

At eight, my friends and I were talking just outside the condemned apartment in which Mama and I lived and would stay as long as we could because the rent was cheap. "You live there? How can you stand it?"

With a shrug and a shake of their heads, they wandered off to their freshly painted, sunny four rooms and bath. *Not as good as other people.* From their casual remarks, their inclusions and exclusions, acceptances and prejudices, wisdoms and stupidities, what I saw in their eyes and heard in their voices, I formed a perception of who I was. And I didn't like what I saw. So I denied her existence and wore a series of roles as my "self" instead.

SHAPING OUR SELF-CONCEPTS

We begin to build images of ourselves from the time we lay in our cribs cooing and gooing. Did Mama coo back? Did she change our diapers tenderly? Did she caress us while we sucked? Were we praised, "Good girl!" when we patted Kitty instead of pulling her ears?

People wandered in and out of our lives and shaped concepts of who we are. There was the boy who loved us in second grade and the girl who refused to be our friend. The coach who said we had promise and the music teacher who said we were tone deaf. The cousins/aunts/neighbors . . . "You're pretty/ugly; agile/clumsy; like the rest of us/different; competent/helpless; wanted/unwanted." If our fathers praised us for playing a new piano piece, we felt good about ourselves. If he screamed across the kitchen table, "Why can't you get an A in math? You're stupid, that's why!" We nodded solemnly behind our faces and built "stupid" into our perception of ourselves.

HOW MY OWN SELF-IMAGE WAS FORMED

Some of the people who moved in and out of my own life, especially when I was a teen, seemed to infer that I was what I wore—a fifty cent sweater and shoes that were too wide but cheap. Bargain table dresses—two for my freshman year; both identical plaid—one blue, the other green.

My value seemed to be reflected in the food I ate, too. County welfare provided vouchers instead of money for mother and me to turn in at the grocery store. Meals were stark: for breakfast, oatmeal or Wheatena; for lunch, a jam sandwich or a mayonnaise and relish sandwich across from kids in the school cafeteria who were biting into roast beef and ham.

I was poor, so I was different. My father was a Jew, so I was different. I was different because my father was insane. To visit Daddy, I boarded a Long Island Railroad train with my mother and traveled to the Northport, N.Y. Veteran's Hospital where he was kept locked up. Other fathers came home from work at five o'clock and asked "How was school today?" and then sat in the living room and read the *Brooklyn Eagle* until supper.

Every rejection reinforced my perception of the truth: some people had worth; I did not. Vicki did: she sang with a band and wore sweaters and skirts marked *best* in the *Sears* catalog. Wanda did. She lived in a big white house and had pound cake for breakfast. Her father went to a job five mornings a week and worked in their garden on Saturday.

What often emerges when we build our self-image haphazardly (because we know no other way), is an out-of-kilter tower like the one our toddler builds of blocks. Sometimes ours teeters, too, threatening to crash, and we hold our breath. That the information we use to build a self-image is not necessarily the truth about who we are, we have no way to tell. For we are toddlers ourselves.

THE KIND OF EXPERIENCES THAT SHAPE OUR SELF-IMAGE

Our conclusions about who we are become the skeleton of our self-image. The experiences that provide the bones for our particular skeleton varies, but they fall into some general categories.

Economic. Unstylish clothes. Thrift store furniture in a cheap apartment when others live in big houses with furniture that matches. Bargain table income and an identity to match.

Ethnic and racial. Dumb Polack, money hungry

Kike, dirty Hymie, shanty Irish, Nigger, Chink. "Because I'm a full-blooded Indian, most people didn't know how to relate to me," a young woman told me. "So I built a wall and shut them out."

Parental. Compared with siblings. Ignored. Called "stupid kid." A mama who sleeps until noon and watches soaps until four. A daddy who sits in the living room in his underwear, even when your friends come. Drunken brawls that wake you, terrified, when it's dark outside. Deserted. Neglected.

Social. Sheltered, like my friend Mary. "My Dad is very shy. We never went to visit other's homes, just stayed on the farm except for school, church on Sunday, and anything else absolutely necessary." In high school Mary felt so different from her peers she became terrified of them.

Developmental. "My mother beat me," Julie told me. "How can you accept yourself when your own mother doesn't?"

Physical. Big ears. Ugly teeth. Lila was a fat baby and a fat girl. She became a fat woman. Although she's thin now, in her head she's "Fat Lila, look at her waddle."

Intellectual. She came to me for help. "I've written lots of articles, but I can't submit them to a magazine. I can't stand rejection. My Dad told me over and over when I was growing up that I was just plain stupid. My husband always protected me. Now I'm alone and I feel completely incapable." She was seventy-years-old.

Religious. Saturday Skool instead of Sunday School. Catholic when most are Protestant; Protestant when most are Catholic. Convinced that Christians are to consider themselves as "nothing," devoid of personhood, so God could take them over.

Sexual. Molested. Raped. *How could I have let it happen? It must have been my fault. I'm bad.*

THE NECESSITY OF SELF-WORTH

Christians whose images are intact sometimes cluck "Shame, shame," at us. "All this talk about self-image is sanctified self-centeredness." They fail to understand.

"A woman with an inferiority complex will have as many problems relating to God and others as an egotistical woman. . . . It is vitally important to a woman's spiritual sense of well-being . . . to accept herself in a wholesome, balanced way."[1] A self-deprecating woman will never have confidence enough to believe she can live in a loving inner union with God and, out of that union, be able to move as a whole person in her world.

Perhaps our critics have confused self-worth with pride; perhaps we've done so ourselves. *Self-worth* is the intrinsic value one places on oneself. *Pride* is a sense of one's own importance apart from God.

Many of us have been continually measuring our worth by comparing ourselves to our peers, seeing their big houses and our shacks, their sober parents and our drunken ones. Our self-image, says Josh McDowell, is the set of lenses through which we view reality.

Without self-worth, some of us assume protective mechanisms like hognosed snakes who freeze when they are approached and, if pressed, hiss and flatten their necks pretending to be cobras. We raise pseudo heads to our enemies like lantern bugs to deflect fatal bites to our egos.

We feel unloved so we become gift-givers, or insecure so we become hoarders; we feel inferior so we become defensive, sharp-tongued cynics, underachievers or overachievers, or Christian legalists. We withdraw, wear masks, grovel in pretended humility, hide in fear or snarl in anger, rejecting people before they reject us. We may even eat moths. Peter Ford, son of actor Glenn Ford and dancer Eleanor Powell did. "I'll give you fifty cents if you eat that moth," another student in study hall told him. "I ate the moth. I did it to be different. To be special. To be noticed because I was me."[2]

Journal Exercise: Write about two experiences that caused you to form a negative image of yourself. What attitudes toward yourself did you develop as a result? What feelings and behavioral patterns? Were your conclusions faulty? Why?

SIN DISTORTS OUR PERCEPTION

Our molders and shapers may have steered us wrongly, leading us to believe we were inferior in some way. Probably, though, they were doing the best they knew how. I didn't mean to mislead my own sons about their true worth while they were growing up. But nevertheless, I did, because my own thinking process about human identity was confused. Sin has distorted the way all of us see ourselves. Parents who feel inferior themselves, for example, probably do not have the capacity to make their offspring feel confident. Or they may build into their children an inflated idea of their capabilities to which they can never measure up.

Others, like a girl I know, pull us down to lift themselves up. She taunted me about the clothes I wore because she felt inferior and tearing me down made her feel better.

Part of the fault for the distorted images we form is our own. Because of sin, we are always comparing ourselves to others to see if we rate better or worse. Walk into a store in your best black shirtwaist dress with your hair freshly done and meet an acquaintance in snagged polyester pants and raincoat with a grease stain down the front, and your self-worth shoots up perceptibly. But if you are the woman in the polyester pants and raincoat and she is the one in the black shirtwaist dress, your self-worth plummets to the basement.

THE END OF FRAGMENTATION

These unbiblical concepts of who we are can go on controlling our attitudes, emotions, and behavior for our entire lives. That's probably what would have happened to me if I hadn't become exhausted from dragging my distorted sense of self, like a dirty childhood bundle, and screamed to God for help.

To whom else should we go for identification? For we are not unnamed creatures of chance waiting to be defined by every passerby. We are God's workmanship created in Christ Jesus.

God is our Architect. Only he can tell us who we really are.

1. Joanne Coughran, "Learning to Love Yourself,"*Virtue*, May/June 1980, p. 68.

2. Raymond Strait, *Hollywood's Children* (New York: St. Martin's Press, 1982), p. 41.

LIKE FATHER, LIKE DAUGHTER

W e were beginners in Sunday school when we first recited our identity. *God made the world and God made me.*

Hard as we tried to keep that as our whole truth, the existentialist concept of human as machine permeated our thinking. We turned away quickly and sang our choruses more loudly, but still we found ourselves feeling a little less human.

Then a nun in Calcutta came along and reminded us of what it means to be human. Her message in action was so startling the world applauded and gave her the Nobel Prize. *Mankind is made in the image of God,* Mother Theresa and her sisters imply as they cradle dying beggars in their arms. *Each, therefore, is of inestimable value.*

Their words are an echo from Eden when our Creator himself whispered our name, *image of God.* He wrote it in Scripture, so anyone through the centuries who came asking who they are, would know. "So God created man in his own image, in the image of God he created him; male and female he created them" (Genesis 1:27).

WHAT IT MEANS TO BE IMAGE OF GOD

James W. Sire describes God's image in us this way. "Man knows himself to be (he is self-conscious), and he makes decisions uncoerced (he possesses self-determination). Man, in other words, is a being capable of acting on his own. He does not merely react to his environment but can act according to his own character."[1]

To be human is to have intelligence (the first human named the animals) and imagination (he dubbed a wiggling creature the polliwog). We are like God because we reason, speak, and put ideas and words together.

We have feelings the way God does, and a will of our own as well. Eve had the independent ability to either resist or yield to sin. Because she was Adam's rib didn't mean she was an inferior creature, able only to choose what Adam would choose. Eve was morally independent, manipulated by no strings.

To be human means to stand on our square foot of earth and choose this or that, say yes or no based on our inner knowledge of right and wrong regardless of our sex. "We are part of the holy mysteries . . . But we are to show our obedience to Aael through this—never eating the fruit,"[2] Risha told Shia in Harold Myra's biblical novel based on Eden.

EXPERIENCING QUALITIES OF THE IMAGE OF GOD

I keep forgetting to appreciate that I am made in the image of God. Yesterday, though, God reminded me of it again.

After I finished researching at the library, I walked toward town through the park. The sidewalk took me alongside a manmade lake and waterfalls. On a bench in a sheltered grove, I sat and studied the vines that served as a ground cover. Showing among them (like lavender and yellow smiles) were crocuses. In February. I imagined myself touching a pistil and coming away with orange fingers. The moment was a memory I could carry with me. (But I could not carry a crocus, for picking was against the law.)

As I got up to walk the path, I realized that this was part of what it feels like to be a human made in the image of God. Smelling and seeing February, calling flowers by name, choosing not to pick, imagining what it would be like to slide down falls riding only on the water's skin. Self-awareness that I am Marion Duckworth and that I am sitting in the park on a warm February day.

I am image of God. Likeness of the Divine. How could I have taken that for granted?

THE MIRACLE OF BEING A WOMAN

After I left the park, I waited at a corner for a walk signal and thought ahead. When I got home, I'd sauté the zucchini and check the refrigerator for leftovers to go with dinner . . . see what time Jack wanted to eat.

As I crossed the street, I chuckled. Suddenly I was thinking like Marion, the woman, I realized. "Male and female created he them." Likeness of God, species called mankind, created of the sex called female. Most of us take this wonder of our gender for granted. Or we think of breasts in terms of nursing or sexiness or cancer, and ovulation in terms of "Could I be pregnant?" Our femaleness is a given, like our family name.

When in our lives do we stop simply responding to the gong of our biological clock and appreciate who we are? To do so requires initiative. It's easier just to keep busy being female, to become absorbed with love, engagement and marriage, pregnancy, childbirth, motherhood, and menopause.

God created me female so I fell in love with Irving when I was seven. At twelve, I lay down in our Coney Island apartment with cramps, fell asleep a girl and awoke a woman. I discovered *boys*. Ralph down the block who played the saxophone.

Not even after I became a Christian did I take time to learn about the wonders of my own femaleness. Not once did I stand before the mirror appreciating my naked self (ignoring the extra pounds for the moment), imagining the parts I knew were inside. I simply accepted my gift and put it on without inspecting its intricacies or thanking God for his craftmanship while continuing to appreciate it as an object d'art.

God created us female! Celebrate! "Sing to the Lord a new song, for he has done marvelous things; . . . Shout for joy to the Lord . . . burst into jubilant song with music" (Psalm 98:1 and 4) For humanness, for femaleness. In the park and in the bathtub.

Journal Exercise: Ponder Psalm 139:13 and 14. Think of two ways that you, as a woman, are fearfully and wonderfully made. How does this make you feel about yourself? About God?

WE ARE INDIVIDUALS

But we aren't just a human female seated on a park bench. We are *this particular* human. "Apart from identical twins, no two individuals are exactly alike. . . . Each individual inherits such a number of diverse chemical markers from his parents and ancestors that he cannot but be . . . unique. . . . Each of us is an original composition."[3]

It wasn't God's intention to bring into existence a race of perfect "10's" with chiseled features and flawless bodies according to the specs of some ad agency. He doesn't read *Vogue* and design hourglass figures or tall, clotheshorse types to suit the era.

His priority is individuality, each person uniquely designed from a combination of inherited characteristics and through their developmental process. From the inside out, we are only ourselves. Our peculiar national, physiological, psychological, and personality traits distinguish us from others. (Nose like Mama's, hunger to know like Daddy; good in English, poor in math; easily moved like Grandpa who shed tears when he heard the Lone Ranger cry "heigh ho, Silver" on the radio.)

INDIVIDUALS IN INTIMACY

God created us uniquely, not only because he is creative and loves variety, but also so that he can have unique relationships with each of us. Because each human personality is different, each relationship is different.

God has intimate relationships with millions of individuals, but none replaces the one with us. A friend illustrated that point when she told me about her experience after her son was taken in crib death. "Several months later, my husband and I adopted a child. Then I became pregnant and we had a biological child. *But neither of them replaced the child who had died.* One child simply does not replace another. I'll always have a special place for the one who's gone to be with God."

God has a special place for each of us. That's why he took our sins in his body when he was crucified. Not just those of a group of elites. Ours.

Jesus Christ acted as mediator, making reunion with the Father possible. When we return, like prodigal daughters, God throws his arms around us, kisses us, and invites us to live in filial union with him. Now, in the sanctuary called our spirit—not just later in a mansion in heaven.

So long as we identify ourselves by our relationships to other people, by our roles and accomplishments, we women *will* be fragmented. Wholeness comes when we see ourselves the way Jesus did. His true identity wasn't carpenter or itinerant preacher or son of Mary and Joseph. His true self resided in his interior, inseparable, eternal union with his heavenly father.

That's the identity he came to give us. Life, he called it—the integration of our spirit center with God who is Spirit, so that his life energizes all of our faculties. When we learn to live out of our Spirit/spirit center, the press of the multitudes and Pharisee's barbs will not shatter us, for our real self will remain in him.

But our spiritual selves seem nebulous, hard to know. Mostly our lives center on the concrete. *Take mother to the supermarket at four, dinner on by six, hem my blue dress before bedtime.* So we resort to the concrete for fulfillment.

However, educational degrees, promotions to executive level, weekly appointments at the beauty salon, and a fat clothing allowance do not in themselves make us whole women. Not even doing Christian things in evangelical churches does it for us.

Only union with the Shepherd can. "Follow after me," he says, "and you shall lack nothing. Let me teach you how to live in the green pastures and quiet waters of your reborn spirit. Let me restore your soul."

Journal Exercise: Gain new appreciation of yourself as a creature made in the image of God. Choose two of the following and write about them.

1. Use your ability to think and reason by writing a paragraph that tells why you do/do not believe in abortion.

2. Use your imagination to recreate Matthew 14:22-33. Write a paragraph putting yourself in the scene.

3. Use your ability to choose by deciding to do an act of kindness that is hard for you to do. Write about how you made the choice and carried it through.

4. Write about a recent experience that evoked strong feelings of love or gratitude in you.

After each exercise, ponder the process that allowed you to do it. After each exercise, write your response.

1. James W. Sire, *The Universe Next Door* (Downer's Grove, Ill.: Inter-Varsity Press, 1979), p. 29.

2. Harold Myra, *The Choice* (Wheaton, Ill.: Tyndale House, 1980), p. 28.

3. Jean Hamburger, M.D., *Discovering the Individual* (New York: W.W. Norton & Co., Inc., 1978), p. 28, 38, 40.

THE PERSON
BENEATH
MY SKIN

Until I was thirty years old, "The Lord is my Shepherd" were only pretty words I memorized in church school. When I said them in class they were soothing. But afterward, the feeling faded and the words settled in the folds of my brain beside the capital of Switzerland and the pledge of allegiance. So far as I could tell, no shepherd was leading and restoring me.

The words stayed handy in my head and I said them when I grew up and was scared because I had to stay alone all night. But no place inside me affirmed "Yes. The Shepherd's here."

That's because the part of me that could know him was dead. But I had no idea that was true. There were no physiological symptoms that anything was wrong—no paralysis or disfunctioning organ, no withered arm or leg, no physical numbness. No internal disharmony awoke me at night.

Certainly I looked and acted like other women I knew. Like them, I worked all day, settled on the sofa in the evening with my husband to watch a TV show, perhaps eat an extra dessert, perhaps make love.

I did notice *something* wrong, but I told myself that was how it was with everyone. The vague, disturbing sense of wrongness came on me every evening about 11:00 P.M. That's when Jack and I would make sure the door was locked, the gas stove was off, the boys safe in their beds, and make our way into our own tiny back bedroom.

We were like children with lollipops, trying to make the ending minutes of the evening last as long as we could. Undressing, getting into bed, he spoke a fragment of a sentence and I spoke one back. "Sure was nice . . . love you . . . love you, too." Then silence as we prayed.

I never dared sleep without saying the words, "I lay me down to go to sleep; I pray thee Lord my soul to keep." I tried saying the prayer as many ways as I knew how: with intensity, pounding key words to heaven with a thrust of emotion; repeating them in a manufactured childlikeness; desperately pleading that God would keep my soul or, if I died before morning, take it to heaven. It was during the saying of that prayer that I sensed something must be wrong. For no matter how I said the words, they bounced against the ceiling like tennis balls.

There *was* a God; I knew that. Was he playing cosmic hide and seek or hadn't I gotten the knack of praying to him yet? Was he a feudal lord who demanded obeisance but wouldn't let vassels like me close enough to touch him? I was caught between two impossibilities: of saying the prayer and hoping that it would be heard, or not saying it and risking hell.

I made the choice with the least risk—to keep saying prayers like grade school recitations of historical data ("Columbus discovered America in 1492") in order to get good marks and please the big people. But now I was one of the big people and I ached for more than rote.

I know now that others have been as confused over the deadness of their prayers as I was—that they are frowning into the darkness thinking vaguely, *something's wrong*.

And we are all correct. Our words are dead because we are dead. But we can't perceive our condition, because we live in a world where deadness is normal.

We aren't corpses in coffins deteriorating into dust and skeletal remains. Deadness exists inside our bodies in the place from which our prayer originates and where we can know God intimately—our spirit.

We are without life. There is simply an absence of God and his life within, a result of our separation from him due to our sin.

SPIRIT IS THE ESSENCE OF GOD

We want to understand more precisely. *Define spirit. What is its substance? Where is it in the human frame?*

45

Spirit cannot be defined so we can understand it. Like the infant who cannot comprehend photosynthesis, we do not yet have the capacity. The human spirit does not come with a label of its ingredients.

But the dimension called spirit that aches to hear whispers from heaven does exist. It is referred to in the Bible as a separate, specific part of a human.

"The [Holy] Spirit himself testifies with *our spirit* that we are God's children" (Romans 8:16, italics mine).

"May your whole *spirit*, soul and body be kept blameless at the coming of our Lord Jesus Christ" (1 Thessalonians 5:23, italics mine).

Man's spirit, according to Watchman Nee, is the element in him that produces God-consciousness. God who is Spirit created man to have a spirit. Because of that similarity in our natures, we can experience intimacy.

OUR SPIRIT MUST BE REBORN

For communication to take place, our spirit must receive God's life. For me, that took place in Flushing, N.Y., when I was nearly thirty years old. "We search for God because we were created to know him," the minister in my new church said. "But we're born dead—separated from God because of our sin.

"Agree in prayer today that you're a sinner and invite Jesus Christ to be your personal Savior. He paid in his own body for your sins. The moment you do that, God will give your own spirit new life, and his Holy Spirit will come in and live there. From that moment on, you'll have a personal relationship with God. You'll be his child."

At home, I kneeled. I prayed. In the seconds it takes a spark to ignite, I knew. I had become alive.

SPIRITUAL LIFE AFFIRMED

Only after God's life comes into our spirit can we understand that spiritual dimension. We must experience life before we can compare it with death. Women have wombs, but until life is conceived in them, they have no consciousness of the organ's existence. But when sperm fertilizes ovum, when embryo forms and grows to become a fetus, she knows: *there is life in my womb*.

John's Gospel affirmed that I'd read my signs of life correctly. He wrote that spiritual birth was as real as physical. He quoted Jesus in John chapter 3, saying that whoever puts their trust in the Son is born a second time in an instantaneous, inner birth. "That which is begotten partakes of the nature of that which begat it,"[1] Olshausen says. The children I carried in my womb possessed a human nature like me because Jack and I, both humans, conceived it. My spiritual life possesses God's nature. "Flesh gives birth to flesh, but the Spirit gives birth to spirit" (John 3:6).

"God has given us eternal life," John writes, "and this life is in his Son. He who has the Son has life; he who does not have the Son of God does not have life" (1 John 5:11 and 12).

Over and over, God repeats the word: *Life*. We have *life*. Women who have been born from above have eternally alive spirits, united with God in intimacy now and forever and ever, Amen.

Journal Exercise: Write a letter to your Heavenly Father in celebration of your rebirthday—that day when your spirit became alive. Recall details of the experience—how you personally asked Christ into your life, how you first began to experience intimacy with him. Thank him. Make your letter a joyful reminiscence.

If you only know about God but do not know him personally because you've never been spiritually reborn, tell him that. Would you like to live in intimacy with him? Invite Jesus into your life. Your prayer should contain the following ideas.

"I want you to live in me. I'm not pure like you are. Forgive me for the things I've done wrong because of my self-centeredness. Thanks for living a perfect life for me and for dying for me, too. Come into my life."

Record your rebirth in your journal. Then write 1 John 5:12 and call it your new birth announcement.

MEET THE WOMAN WHO IS NEVER FRAGMENTED

That inner spiritual woman who has been reborn and is indwelled with God is your true self. She is the one who can never be fragmented because she is integrated into the eternal God—the I Am—who will keep her. Real life isn't a jogger's high, she knows now. It is called "abundant, eternal life" by Jesus.

"True personhood does not require a body," David Needham explains. It is intangible and eternal. Paul was anxious to die and be with God, Needham reminds us. Was that apostle wishing to become a nonperson?[2]

A woman's reborn spirit, though intangible, has substance. In that dimension she has a sixth sense called knowing, the result of the illumination of her spirit by God's Spirit. Through that sixth sense she can communicate with him—she can talk with God, know that he hears, and sense his inaudible answer. "Ears that hear," Jesus called that perceptiveness. (Not to be confused with that vagary called women's intuition.)

Peter Virtue is a deaf Christian who understands this sense. When he prayed to be healed "so I can hear the music in church," God answered. "You can already hear. You are talking to me and understand what I am saying. It is more important to hear spiritually than physically."[3]

In her spirit, this woman understands what it means to be holy, as though she'd grown spiritual antennae. There she can learn to perceive the nature of God and be energized by him. She can experience his desires, a Divine sense of purpose, and a determination to persevere.

As a result of her spiritual fusion with God, she can express his nature—his qualities—through her own personality and character. She can demonstrate the peace and patience, joy and love that exists internally in him—even when kids whine or customers crowd her counter two minutes before closing time. Her spiritual self can "rejoice, grieve, anticipate, love, fear, approve, condemn, decide, discern."[4]

Journal Exercise: Exercise the faculties of your spirit in two of the following ways.

1. Write a paragraph telling how you sensed God's answer when you prayed about a particular problem.

2. Write about one way God has convicted you to be more like him.

3. Ask God to enable you to express one of his qualities in a difficult situation. Write about the experience.

The inner house called our spirit where we once existed alone is now alive and echoes with love, faith, and hope. Because that's true, we are finding that fulfillment is not a clause in our marriage contract or a bonus accompanying our paycheck.

Fulfillment is living with Jehovah in our sanctuary. Just as the holy of holies—that inner room where God's presence lived and where he met with the high priest—was the sanctuary of the Old Testament temple, so a woman's spirit is her sanctuary.

But we are not like those priests who went into the stone temple's most sacred room to minister before God, then had to leave his presence to minister to people in the outer court, taking with them only the glow. We live with him permanently in the sanctuary of our spirit.

Because that's true, we can remain whole while we swab up water after the toilet overflows, while we confront the Pharisees of our lives, or as we take little children on our lap.

1. *Jamison, Fausset & Brown's Commentary on the Whole Bible*, vol. 5, (Glasgow, 1863), p. 362.

2. David Needham, *Birthright* (Portland, Or.: Multnomah Press, 1979), p. 88.

3. "Minister Finds Blessing in Deafness," *Statesman* (Salem, Oregon), 26 May 1984.

4. Watchman Nee, *The Spiritual Man*, vol. 2, (New York: Christian Fellowship Publications, Inc., 1968), p. 70.

FALLING
IN LOVE

The idea of living in spiritual wedlock with God Almighty through a personal relationship with Jesus Christ can seem like a biblical Hans Christian Anderson tale—even to the spiritually reborn. Some days intimacy in the sanctuary of one's spirit can seem to be reserved for Ruth Bell Graham and Elisabeth Elliot or those Christian women whom we imagine live in a celestial-like environment.

Your spiritual woman may still be a weak, ghostly figure that is barely recognizable and certainly unable to support your weight. You try to beef her up the way you try to diet—irregularly. But you have little time or energy left after struggling sixteen hours-a-day to keep your job and care for your family. So you remain a perfect "before," and the contrast to the Scriptural "after" makes you sick.

For years I existed in that state of low-grade nausea over my unsatisfactory relationship with God. No weekend spiritual athlete, I performed all the right Christian calisthentics rigorously. I read the Bible and other important Christian books; participated in church life, prayed, and tried to obey the commandments as I understood them.

Still there seemed to be a partition in my spiritual sanctuary. The intimacy I read about in John's Gospel— "he in me and I in him"—wasn't coming true for me. Walking in the Holy Spirit was a Rubic's cube I couldn't solve.

Scripture said my inner woman was joined in union with Jesus Christ, but I sensed no happily ever after. If ours had been a marriage of convenience because I wanted assurance of eternal security, the distance between us would have been easier to understand. Or if I'd accepted Christ the way a friend became a Missus: "Everyone was getting married, so I did, too," it would have been easier to fathom.

No matter what motivated us to receive the Son, his motive for coming into our lives is always love. Long before we knew him, he was speaking tenderness to us. But perhaps we didn't hear. Perhaps we've never heard because we've been dazzled by his wealth or the power he wields or the mansions he promised.

Or perhaps after the two of us became one, a career or a child died and he seemed not to care, so we turned away. Maybe we married a man that fit none of our girlhood fantasies or have found no man to marry and the ache has been all we can think about. *If God loved me, he'd change things.*

Or anniversaries have piled up since our union with God, and now we take his presence for granted and sit across from him in silence, performing our duties and thinking bittersweet memories of the way things used to be. Instead of a sanctuary continually filled with God's glory, our spirit is like the one I attended when I was a teenager where sounds of worship could be heard only on Sunday at eleven.

Others have told me how they've struggled to believe in God's love. A grandmotherly woman sat next to me on a sofa in a conference grounds lounge crying because, though she'd known Christ personally for decades, she still couldn't believe that he loved her. A few years before a young wife had sat across the kitchen table from me toying with her teacup. She was an earnest Christian—first in line for voluntary service—but God seemed as distant from her as her own father had been.

An entire nation refused to believe God's confession of love and went whoring after other gods. Their history is described in the Old Testament. "God has chosen you out of all the peoples on the face of the earth to be his people, his treasured possession," Moses wrote. And "Israel joined in worshiping the Baal of Peor. And the Lord's anger burned against them" (Deuteronomy 7:6, Numbers 25:3).

GOD'S LOVE IS A CLICHÉ

The facts are clear in Scripture. "He first loved us" (1 John 4:19). But "God loves you" has become a cliché. It slides across our brain and never takes root. It leers at us from little smiling faces and stares at us on bumpers in traffic jams. We pin it in gold to our lapels.

The church has sloganned the love of God as though it was selling Pepsi. Secularists, on the other hand, have reduced the loving God to a poetic abstract. "We can anticipate the time in the history of the human race," writes Erich Fromm, "when God ceases to be an outside power, where man has incorporated the principles of love and justice into himself, where he has become one with God, and eventually, to a point where he speaks of God only in a poetic, symbolic sense."[1]

The church manages to get us singing the jingle and wearing the jewelry, but somehow we do not believe the truth. It is easier to believe what the absence of God in our secularized society implies: His love is a pleasant myth. Or that it is abstract, the way God himself seems to be.

Journal Exercise: Think of two people who have told you they love you. How did you know they meant it? Now think of one Bible verse and one hymn in which God's love is mentioned. Does that seem just as real? If not, why? How has this affected your relationship with God?

GOD LOVES MANKIND

God does declare in the Scripture that he loves mankind, both men and women. His is *agapaō* love. "It springs from an apprehension of the preciousness of an object . . . is determined by the character of the one who loves . . . the degree of the preciousness is measured by the infinite sacrifice which God made."[2]

What does that kind of love look like? I asked some women in a Bible study I taught when in their lives they'd seen love. "Because," I added, "whenever we experience unselfish, sacrificial love, we are seeing a reflection of the love of God himself."

One woman answered, "When I was in my teens, I didn't get along with my stepfather. But I became very sick and lay in bed drifting in and out of consciousness. Every time I'd open my eyes, I saw my stepfather there at the foot of my bed. He had the most tender look on his face! I found out later that he stayed with me all that time. That's when I knew, *he loves me.*

God is like that father. For centuries, he's been waiting at the foot of mankind's sickbed.

THE NAMES OF GOD REVEAL HIS LOVE

The very names he's used to introduce himself to us describe him, not only as Love, but as one who wishes to direct that love toward the human race.

Here are some of those names in the Old Testament:

Jehovah-jireh—the self-existent one will provide;

Jehovah-rophe—the self-existent one heals;

Jehovah-rohi—the self-existent one, my shepherd;

Jehovah-tsidkenu—the self-existent one, our righteousness;

Jehovah-shammah—the self-existent one is there.[3]

"When Christianity says that God loves man, it means that God *loves* man . . . you asked for a loving God; you have one . . . not a senile benevolence . . . but the consuming fire Himself."[4]

A BIBLICAL MONTAGE OF GOD'S LOVE

Recently I saw a one-minute history of America on television. Edited together in a fast-flicking montage were scenes like settlers at Plymouth Rock, the Boston tea party, a Civil War battle, the raising of the flag on Iwo Jima, race riots, Nixon's resignation.

Imagine that the following is the script for a film like that one. Play it in your mind and see once and for all whether or not God has demonstrated irrefutably that he loves mankind.

Scene one: God in Eden on the dawn of the sixth day, creating the man and woman so he'd have creatures with whom to fellowship forever. Adam and Eve choose their meal from among the vegetation in God's garden that had been created as a perfect environment for them. They pause to scratch a giant cat's ear.

Scene two: The man and woman crouch in hiding from God because they've sinned. He finds them and promises to send a Savior.

Scene three: The ancient world has become a porno strip. God warns. He commands Noah to build an ark and offers safety from the coming destruction to any who are repentant. Not until the ark doors close does the promised deluge begin. The remnant of the people God created in his image float in safety.

Scene four: God picks out one man and woman, Abraham and Sarah, to father and mother a nation that would be called "my people." Through them he'd show himself to the world. To them he reveals his law, gives a land in which to live, a way of forgiveness and worship; to them he makes promises of perpetual care as long as they obey him; among them he'd come to live. "The glory of Lord filled the tabernacle" (Exodus 40:35). *God among men.*

At peace in her land but as restless as a spoiled child, Israel runs with neighbor children to Baal and Molech. God mourns. "When Israel was a child, I loved him . . . but the more I called Israel, the further they went from me." But he promises: "I will heal their waywardness and love them freely." (Hosea 11:1 and 2; 14:4).

Scene five: A stable in Nazareth during the national census. Out from a virgin and covered with membrane and blood, God the Son is born. God among men.

See him as obedient Jewish child, as carpenter, as itinerant preacher. Watch him heal. Hear him declare himself "The way, the truth, the life." See him arrested because he said "I and the Father are one." Watch him on trial, beaten, bleeding, and silent; then suffocating on the cross, nails tearing him. See him slump in death.

See the stone rolled away, the tomb empty, Jesus standing alive outside. Hear him tell Thomas, "Reach out your hand and put it into my side. Stop doubting and believe" (John 20:27).

Scene six is in Jerusalem where one hundred twenty believers are worshiping. Like a mighty wind, God's Spirit comes in fulfillment of Jesus' promise. "I will not leave you as orphans; I will come to you" (John 14:18). Watch those believers and countless others through the centuries whom God fills with his presence, calls "Christ's body on earth," and sends to the whole world so he can bear more children to love.

But the body grows lazy, fattened on its neighbor. Bloody wars are bannered in his name. Christ becomes curse. Still he stays.

Scene seven is as bright as glistening gold, a "city (that) does not need the sun or the moon to shine on it, for the glory of God gives it light." He speaks the final words, "'Come!' . . . Whoever is thirsty, let him come; and whoever wishes, let him take the free gift of the water of life. . . . I am coming soon" (Revelation 21:23; 22:17 and 20).

The film has ended, but its images linger. *Who is pursuer? Who is pursued? Mankind or Godhead?*

Have we supposed that because we picked our way through religions to find God and invited him into our lives that we were the aggressors? Or can we admit that we found him because he sought us from the beginning and his love drew us to him?

Replay the film. Stop anywhere—in Hosea, perhaps, where God longs for mankind the way a husband longs for a wife who has deserted him. Or in Matthew where God the Son is talking to the crowds and his disciples. "O Jerusalem, Jerusalem . . . how often I have longed to gather your children together, as a hen gathers her chicks under her wings, but you were not willing" (Matthew 23:37).

Journal Exercise: Write a letter to a non-Christian friend (You will keep it in your journal). Tell him or her all the ways you can think of that God has proven his love for the human race.

GOD LOVES WOMAN

God not only loves mankind. He loves each man and woman.

My friend Harriet can't believe God loves her. One reason is because she is a woman. To her husband, femaleness is synonymous with temptress, so she can never be submissive enough. Like many of her sisters, she has been defined more as a utensil to be kept in her place than as a person to be loved.

Jesus Christ did not so define women. He ministered regardless of sex. He sat with Mary to explain the Kingdom to her. At a well he talked with a Samaritan woman, telling her how to find eternal life. The Son of God had no part in a religion that subjugates women. In the kingdom of God, women are not worth half the price of a man (the way they are in the kingdom of the Ayatollah).

The church of Jesus Christ is neither Jew nor Greek, bond nor free, and neither is it male nor female. Man and woman have been created in the image of God. Both were instructed to subdue the earth. Both were called to repentance, invited to receive eternal life, indwelt by the Spirit of God, made joint heirs with Christ and members of his body. Both have been given gifts with which to minister to that body.

GOD LOVES INDIVIDUALS

We nod in quick assent. *Absolutely. God does love woman.* He showed in the Bible that he isn't an impersonal Deity who blesses the masses. He is a personal God who has relationships with men and women with frailties just like ours.

But there's a big difference between agreeing that the facts are true and believing that they are true of me. *God loves this woman, this person inside my skin.*

But how can he? we object. After all, I'm inconsistent, quick-tempered, selfish, resentful . . .

God helped me see the fallacy of my reasoning recently when I saw Phil Nash of The Dramatic Word put on his one-man performance of 2 Timothy, "Come Before Winter."

Portraying the aged Paul, Phil knelt on a nearly-bare stage that represented the cold, rock dungeon in which the apostle was imprisoned when he wrote that epistle. "Do your best to come to me quickly," he implored. "Only Luke is with me . . . When you come, bring the cloak that I left with Carpus at Troas, and my scrolls, especially the parchments" (4:9-13).

Paul was human like me. He had his own weaknesses. Sure, he was male, not female, and wore a robe, not a gabardine suit. He lived in the first century, not the twentieth, and was a tentmaker and apostle, not writer, wife, and mother. But he was tired, his bones ached . . . he was human like me.

The first century Jews, Greeks, and Romans were not a group of sweepstake winners out of millions of historical entries who were awarded God's love. They were simply the firstborn among many brethren.

1. Erich Fromm, *The Art of Loving* (New York: Bantam Books, 1963), p. 68.
2. Kenneth S. Wuest, "Golden Nuggets,"*Word Studies in the Greek New Testament*, vol. 3, (Grand Rapids: Wm. B. Eerdmans Pub. Co., 1973), p. 60.
3. Nathan J. Stone, *Names of God* (Chicago, Ill.: Moody Press, 1944).
4. C.S. Lewis, *The Problem of Pain* (London: Fontana Books, 1957), p.34, 35.

CONVINCED
BY LOVE

I was just past forty when I realized for the first time that God didn't just love mankind—he loved me. My family and I had just moved to Salem, Oregon, where he led me to a Bible study for women. Marge, the teacher, faced me.

She studied our faces as though beginning a separate conversation with each of us. Finally, she spoke.

"I love you. I want you to know that. I love you and God loves you, too."

God the Holy Spirit confirmed her words to my inner self. *It's true, Marion. Believe her. I do love you.*

God had loved me all along, of course, and had been demonstrating the fact to me through specific acts. But like an ungrateful child, I hadn't been paying attention.

He had been whispering love to me personally and waiting for me to hear and believe him the way Jack did the summer of '48 when we began dating. His words fell softly on my skin, but when I was alone, I paced the room. *Is it really true?* Jack was more handsome and sophisticated than any man I'd known, an actor with a singing voice that boomed the hit tune from a play across the Long Island beach.

He kept affirming his love—writing it every day in letters, showing me by the gifts he gave, proving it through his faithfulness, his acceptance of me even when my hair was in curlers and my nose red from a cold, and by his continual, tender care.

Gradually as we dated, married, and lived together in our one room New York apartment and as I experienced his love, I came to believe him. *He did love me.*

God spoke love the same way. I had believed Jack; I could not believe God.

Even when I did finally believe *God loves me*, I had no idea that he had loved me from the beginning with a depth and persistence I'd never be able to comprehend so long as I was tied to earth.

The incident that made me look more closely at God's love was a discussion following a Bible study I taught. "The older I get," a retired missionary in his eighties commented, "the more I realize how dependent I am on God's grace."

A frail man, he'd lived and worked in Asia most of his life. He still worked daily, translating hymns and Christian literature for people overseas who depended on him. I ranked him with Abraham and Moses.

What was this grace on which he depended? I knew only the number one evangelical definition, "unmerited favor." Obviously, the word had a meaning I hadn't discovered yet. I asked God to help me climb inside the word and look at it with my spirit.

I discovered that, as it applies to God, it means the lovingkindness that causes him to design joy for his creatures. I pictured God the Almighty, great as the universe, bending low to lovingly touch a human tiny as Tim.

"God's grace is that matchless, wonderful, marvelous, act on His part when He out of the spontaneous infinite love of His heart steps down from His judgment throne in heaven to take upon Himself the guilt of our sin and the penalty which is justly ours, doing this not for His friends but for His enemies."[1]

Grace means that God loves me and therefore acts kindly toward me—even though I am completely undeserving. He had demonstrated that in his sacrifice on the cross. But shortsightedly, I'd filed grace away under Ephesians 2:8, "By grace are ye saved" (KJV). The crucifixion was his greatest act of grace, but it certainly wasn't his only one. I hadn't realized that before because I'd never learned to read the sign language of his love.

WHEN GOD STOOPED IN KINDNESS

I began to remember other ways he'd loved me. When I was eighteen years old, I attended a church service in a rented room in a city building. A Jewish evangelist spoke, telling of his conversion to faith in Jesus Christ. Since my own father was a Jew, I was shaken. This man could have been my father. But Daddy was locked in a mental hospital and would never be well enough to respond to a message about Jesus.

When the speaker finished, I raised my hand indicating that I wanted to know Jesus. But after the meeting, no one counseled me. So I dried my eyes and went home and wrote in my Bible the date "When I received Christ." But my response had only been emotional. Within I was still dead.

For twelve years God demonstrated his lovingkindness by drawing me to himself. Once he illuminated Christ through a film about his life. Other times he spoke to me through Christians on the radio.

These acts were the sign language of God's love. Several years ago when I was writing an article about love, I realized when I demonstrate God's love by my actions, I am speaking its sign language.

It took me a lot longer to realize that the kindnesses God performs for us are the sign language of his love.

To retrace the ways he had been acting toward me in love in the past so I'd be more aware of his love in the future, I made a chart. In it I divided my life in segments. In each segment I wrote outstanding ways God performed acts of love in my life.

TIME LINE OF GRACE

To 8th Grade
The teacher who told me when I was 18 that she'd been praying for me since I was in her 2nd grade class

God's care during our years of poverty

Aunts, uncles, and cousins through whom He loved me.

God awakening in me a desire to write

Through High School
A minister who gave me the attention I needed when I was a teen

The Christian music teacher through whom He demonstrated love

God's answer to my mother's prayer that she would live until I became an adult, in spite of her poor health

Two Christian students through whom God revealed Himself

18-30 yrs.
Uniting me with a husband through whom He could show His love

Radio broadcasts through which He told me the Good News

A desire to go to church, the result of early Christian influence

31-40 yrs.
Leading me to an evangelical church

Christians in that church through whom He showed His love

The Holy Spirit drawing me to Christ

A desire and the opportunities to discover and cultivate my gifts

41—
The crisis through which God allowed me to go that forced me to learn about His love

The Bible teacher through whom He spoke love

Other Christians in that group who helped me experience God's love

Provision of experiences through which I learned to live in God's love

God had been loving me all along! First it was *Be my child. Let me father you.* Then, *You are my child. Live believing in my love.*

Not only does God the Father Almighty speak grace historically in acts to the whole world to be appropriated individually like his death for sin, he speaks them privately as well. These are the undeserved acts of kindness he performs for us personally as though he's whispering "I love you," in our ear.

God has always loved us, and he has been vocal about it. His words and his demonstrations of grace prove that.

Learn to see yourself biblically, as loved daughters. Learn to trust in my grace toward you in the future. Learn to live believing in my love.

Journal Exercise: Make your own time line of God's grace. Divide your life into segments similar to those on the chart. Think of ways he acted in kindness toward you during each period. Has God been participating in your life all along? Respond to him.

Once we see how much God loves and values us and that he has been showing us that all along, we begin to value ourselves. *God is the one who determines my worth. He loves and accepts me. It doesn't matter how others see me.* I want them to like and accept me, but if they don't, that doesn't change my estimation of my worth.

When our minds are enlightened by the Holy Spirit enabling us to see that we really do have value to God, we are ready to form a new self-image—one founded on his Word. Instead of theology, the passages in which he describes who we are become love letters. Catching our breath in wonder, we pore over the contents.

"Long ago, even *before he made the world, God chose me to be his very own,* through what Christ would do for me; *he decided then to make me holy in his eyes,* without a single fault—*I who stand before him covered with his love. His unchanging plan has always been to adopt me into his own family* by sending Jesus Christ to die for me. And *he did this because he wanted to!*

"Now all praise to God for *his wonderful kindness* to me and for his favor *that he has poured out upon me* because I belong to his dearly loved son. So overflowing is his kindness towards me that he took away my sins through the blood of his son, by whom I am saved; and he has showered down upon me the richness of his grace. . . . Because of what Christ has done *I have become a gift to God that he delights in,* for as part of God's sovereign plan I was chosen from the beginning to be his, and all things happen just as he decided long ago. God's purpose in this was that I should praise God and give glory to him for doing these mighty things for me. . . .

"Because of what Christ did . . . *I* . . . *was marked as belonging to Christ by the Holy Spirit,* who long ago had been promised to all of us Christians. *His presence within me is God's guarantee that he really will give me all that he promised;* and the Spirit's seal upon me means that God has already purchased me and that he guarantees to bring me to himself. This is just one more reason for me to praise our glorious God" (From Ephesians 1:4-14 TLB, personal pronouns inserted, italics mine).

This is who you are, the Holy Spirit witnessed to my spirit.

> Recipient of every blessing in heaven.
> Chosen to be God's own even before he
>   made the world.
> Made holy in God's eyes, covered with his
>   love.
> Adopted into God's own family.
> One on whom he pours kindness.
> Forgiven.
> Accepted.

A gift in whom he delights.
Indwelt by his Spirit.

Other Scriptures add dimension, and the biblical image of ourselves becomes more clearly defined.

Called friends of Christ (John 15:15).
Lavished with God's love (1 John 3:1).
One who is being recreated in God's image
   (Romans 8:9).
Possesses eternal life (John 10:28).
Has access to wisdom (James 1:5).
Given power by God (Acts 1:8).
Needs met by God (Psalm 37:4).

The image of ourselves we have been carrying around grew out of the mind of a short-sighted world that perceives after the flesh and not the Spirit. It is our spiritual self, created in the image of God, recreated in Jesus Christ, imputed with his righteousness and being honed in the Family image that is our essential, eternal personhood, not our external one.

Our parents may have called us "stupid" or taunted that we were disappointments. Mama may not have seemed to love us, or Daddy, either. We may have compared ourselves to others and felt inferior.

None of these things determine who we are. Not the length of our nose or our stutter or the pronouncement by one of society's self-appointed judges that we deviate from the norm. Any image built on this kind of information is a caricature inspired by Eve's deceiver.

Only the Truth—Elohim himself—can tell us what is true about ourselves, and he has done so. *You are mine. My child, the gift in whom I delight. Accepted just as you are. Forgiven. A temple in which I live.* His words hold a mirror to our spirits; what we see reflected is our true identity.

Journal Exercise: Study your biblical image in Ephesians 1. Think about each statement and talk it over with God. "You have given me every spiritual blessing." What does that imply? "You hear and answer my prayers."

Write your thoughts down and, as you do so, you will be developing a personal, biblical description of who you are. Begin with the following statement. "Only God can tell me who I am. Here's how he describes me."

List some unbiblical ideas about yourself that you have been harboring. Next to them, write the biblical truth that makes your ideas inaccurate. Write your conclusions.

1. Kenneth S. Wuest, "Golden Nuggets," *Word Studies in the Greek New Testament*, vol. 3, (Grand Rapids: Wm. B. Eerdmans Pub. Co., 1973), p. 80.

REMOVING
THE BRICKS

Jane had never built a healthy image of herself. Rejection during her early years had left her feeling unacceptable, unloved, and unlovable. She wrote about her experiences in her journal.

"Once upon a time there was a little girl who grew up in a brick tower. As she grew older, the walls of the tower became higher. There were no windows to let in fresh air or sunshine. She lived in the dark, feeling trapped and helpless.

"Voices from outside occasionally penetrated the thick walls that surrounded her. Once in a while she would pound on them in an effort to attract the attention of someone who might be willing to take the time and trouble to help her find a way out.

"But for many, many years no one heard her cry. People walking by assumed the tower was empty. She grew quieter and quieter so she wouldn't bother anyone. She wasn't important or clever—she felt it would make people angry if they ever discovered her."

Jane finally believed the truth. "One day the miracle began. God shone his light into the darkness of the brick tower and revealed his personal and intimate love for this lonely, desolate girl. She rejoiced to discover the one who loved her so deeply, yet without demands or expectations. She was loved for who she was, not what she was.

"She looked up, amazed. The roof of the tower was gone! Sunshine and fresh air began to penetrate the staleness and gloom. Filled with hope and energy, the girl whom God loved began to remove the bricks, one by one."

TRANSFORMATION THROUGH A RENEWED MIND

Able to see that her old, unbiblical self-concept was distorted, Jane began to build a new image of herself.

Paul describes the process she went through. "Do

not conform any longer to the pattern of this world, but be transformed by the renewing of your mind" (Romans 12:2). "Put off your old self, which is being corrupted by its deceitful desires . . . be made new in the attitude of your minds . . . put on the new self, created to be like God in true righteousness and holiness" (Ephesians 4:22-24).

Be changed, Paul writes. Achieve that change by absorbing into your mind the truth about who you are in Jesus Christ. Learn to see yourself as God sees you and conform your attitudes and behavioral patterns to that new image.

My friend Julie was in her twenties when she began to internalize biblical descriptions of personhood. Rejected by her parents and placed in a series of foster homes, she did not believe she was lovable and capable until she returned to college for her master's degree.

"As I drove back and forth to college, God helped me monitor my thoughts. I was shocked. They were resentful and full of self-pity and fear. I was creating fantasies in which I was the heroine, able to manipulate people to treat me the way I wanted. So when people did not treat me as I'd envisioned, I'd be hurt and angry."

Julie taped a sign, "Think God thoughts," on the dashboard of her car. Whenever she saw herself unbiblically, she'd sense the Holy Spirit's prodding. "God helped me stop conforming to my old pattern of thinking about myself and to change my self-image by renewing my mind. Editing my thoughts is a discipline I'm still practicing."

LET GOD REVEAL HIS LOVE

If feelings of lovelessness have plagued you, confess them to God. *I believe intellectually that you love me because the Bible says so. I do not believe it experientially.* Remember that you cannot convince yourself that God loves you. Only the Holy Spirit can do that.

MEDITATE ON SCRIPTURE

Stop berating yourself. *If I really believed he loves me, I'd trust him wholeheartedly with everything.* Sit regularly in his presence and quietly meditate on Scripture (such as Ephesians 1:1-14) which describes his love for you. (A list in the back of the book provides more passages.) You learn to believe in God's love the way you learn to believe in a parent's love—by listening to their words and paying attention to the sign language of their love.

Learn to see God as he is in Scripture, not as you've imagined him to be. (He is not like your demanding father or your perfectionist mother.) Gradually, in your spiritual self, you will perceive your true identity— beloved daughter of God.

The more you believe in his love for you, the more you'll be able to love him back. Use the words of Psalms like 8 and 145 to tell God you love him when your own words are reluctant to come.

The process of learning about Jesus' love began for Helen several years after her conversion. "Most of it happened when I taught children's classes about God's faithfulness and goodness. I spent time studying and thinking about the lessons; I verbalized the truth out to my class and they verbalized it back to me. The truth about God became firm in my mind.

"I like myself now. I know I can have my own thoughts about things and realize that I may have knowledge that someone else doesn't have. I used to be tied up in knots trying to be all I thought I should be; now I'm able to relax with myself. I'm able to enjoy my children, too. We have more fun than I think we've ever had."

TRUTH MUST BE APPLIED

It is the Holy Spirit's function to affirm to your spirit that you are the one who is loved. *You are my daughter. You are indwelt with my presence, you have been accepted unconditionally. You are the one on whom I am lavishing my*

grace. You can change your attitude and behavior with my guid-
ance and strength.

The more we learn to trust in the depth of God's love for us, the more we can trust him to direct our inner reconstruction process. We are more likely to "tell him our worst thing."

This moment in this place with my uglies on and my back bristled, God loves me. So I can learn to trust him to accept me exactly as I am and commit myself to him to become like he is.

Claire has always had a self-image problem. "My mother raised me to believe that everyone else was better than I. It's my husband who's done the most to help me realize I do have worth and that God loves me.

"I remember going to him to apologize and ask forgiveness for something l said. He responded by saying, 'I already have.' He always says that. I could see that was the way it was with God. He already has."

ASSIMILATE WHO YOU ARE IN CHRIST

Two women in the Bible study where I heard of God's love helped me to assimilate who I am in Christ. We met weekly to talk over our concerns and pray with one another. Until a few years before, one of the women had been fragmented, depending on pills to get her through instead of on her spiritual union with Christ. I could see that she was letting God renew her mind and her behavior. As I experienced God's love through them and saw how he was transforming them, I was able to believe that I could become whole, too.

To heal damaged emotions, one must cultivate healthy relationships. Friendships in which we're accepted by others help us learn to love instead of hate ourselves. Those who value and believe in our abilities encourage us to value and believe in ourselves. So it's imperative that we begin to spend time with people who can do that for us.

It was painfully difficult for me to be open with

others because I was sure they would reject me. Jane felt the same way. But she joined a small group of Christians who met weekly to study Scripture, pray, and help one another grow.

For a long time, she said little in the meetings. Then, as others initiated friendships, she responded (though guardedly at first). They loved her and showed it by the time they spent with her outside the meetings and by acts that demonstrated their concern for her well-being. In a way, they became the loving, accepting intimates she hadn't had earlier in life.

Journal Exercise: Begin your quiet time by telling God everything that's really on your mind. Then meditate on one of the Scriptures that describes the nature of God or his love for you (found in the back of the book). Each day, write a paragraph that describes something new and wonderful about God. Thank him for being this kind of father to you.

PRACTICE THE TRUTH

Learning to live out of your true identity takes practice, just like learning to play the piano. After six lessons we may be able to play "Pop! Goes the Weasel." Tchaikovsky takes more.

God will give us opportunities to change our behavior patterns. When I was on my own journey from fragmentation to wholeness, he sent me to work as a salesclerk to gain confidence in myself and learn relational skills.

Every clerk-customer encounter was a practice session. Dozens of times every day, five days a week, I had to risk rejection. It was as though I'd returned to high school corridors, not as a welfare kid with a Jewish father in an insane asylum, but as a child of God Almighty, Creator of heaven and earth, Amen.

I was afraid. I wanted to quit and run home for safety. But we needed the money, so I had to stay, and in working behind that counter where God put me, I took long strides toward self-love.

Annette began to recover from her poor self-image when she started doing things to like herself. "Before, I was always measuring myself against others. Then I started to learn to look outside myself and concentrate on what was going on around me. Now I make cookies for a friend instead of wishing I was a better friend and feeling worthless."

We must not run from hard things, for they are God's training ground. This is where the transformation process can break down.

But if we keep listening for the Spirit's promptings and promises and set our sights on wholeness, we will persist. We will be able to speak up when it's time for sharing in our Bible study even though we're sure everyone's looking at our big nose. Each sweaty hour we will be aware that God is there to help.

For he's not a father who drops his newborn in the delivery room—*Survive or die*—and strides off to create other worlds. Since before conception in our mothers' wombs he loved us. The years we sat turned away from him, he loved us. And he loves us still.

GIVE YOURSELF TIME

Jane, Julie, and others I know are learning by faith to remove the bricks from their towers—one at a time. Building a new self-image and learning to live out of it takes time.

Learning to handle old feelings takes time. Instead of repressing them, we need to admit them to ourselves and God, and call them by their right name. Fear. Anger. Guilt. And remind ourselves that they are only emotions—responses borne out of our old self-concept. They need not control us.

"Becoming acquainted with healthy feelings is a PROCESS that develops in social relationships and in the flow of daily living. . . . There will be much to learn as the old shell drops away in the day-to-day experience of living, and as the real self comes into its own."[1]

So give yourself time. The more firmly established your habits, the more time you'll need. For me to learn to relate comfortably one-on-one to other people took repeated practice sessions. A key, I discovered, was to confess failure and see every success as an important step toward wholeness.

That process has been working for Mary, too. Her acute shyness which resulted from an extremely sheltered childhood turned her into an adult who hid from passersby behind her living room drapes. After she embraced Christ and was introduced to his love, she accepted an invitation to attend a Christian family camp. But before the week was half over, she ran into the woods and cried to God that she had to go home.

But God didn't want her to give in to her fear and she knew it. So she stayed. Later that week when a teacher in one of the sessions gave Mary a Scripture reference to read aloud during the class, she panicked. Knowing that God wanted her to trust him, she agreed. "I don't know how I'll do it," she prayed. "I may die in the attempt, but I'll try."

Class time ran out before the teacher got to Mary. But through that experience, she realized that her old, inappropriate feelings about herself need not control her actions. She could choose to act out of her biblical image in spite of the way she felt.

Mary's drapes are open now. She visits regularly in a nursing home, teaches junior church, and is a deaconess.

EXPERIENCE CHANGE

As we live in Christ in our spirit, we learn our true identity from him. Our minds absorb that truth, and our attitudes, behavior, and feelings about ourselves and others begin to change.

We grow stronger. More and more the new woman becomes the one in whom we feel at home. Loved, we are motivated to obey God, to outgrow old habits and develop new ones.

"I'm the person you're talking about," said a slender, attractive woman who came up to me after a seminar I taught. "I'm learning to like myself more and more every day. As a matter of fact, I like myself so much that I was able to lose fifty pounds. And even though I never thought of myself as a leader, I'm heading up a weight loss group now."

In summary, the formula by which we can change from fragmented women whose lifestyle is rooted in an unbiblical image to biblical women is this:

Instruction in the correctly interpreted Scripture that states God's unqualified love for you

plus

illumination of those Scriptures by the Holy Spirit in answer to your request

plus

meditation or "controlled thinking" regularly during quiet times by yourself when you muse before God about the meaning of those Scriptures for you

plus

application of the Scriptures to your life. *I am the one on whom God has lavished his grace. I am the one who stands before him covered with his love.*

plus

Assimilation or "to take up and make part of . . . oneself; to incorporate."[2] Continue to make a part of your mindset the truth that you are loved, accepted, and secure. Spend time with people who will reinforce the truth that you are a worthwhile person.

Practice by acting day after day out of the realization that you are God's loved child. Risk rejection and failure. Become vulnerable.

plus

Time. "Don't expect perfection: God doesn't. Don't be discouraged by setbacks. . . . The new personality will not develop all at once."[3] Your old roots may be put down deeply in hard, crusty soil. Give God time to soften the earth and work the roots gradually.

equals

Change. So imperceptibly, perhaps, that no one notices fullness where you were once gaunt. But you know. You spoke up when you once could have been silent; went when you once would have stayed home. God knows, too. You both cheer.

Journal Exercise: What opportunities in your daily life is God giving you to change your behavior? What emotions do you have to deal with? What successes and setbacks have you experienced? Write about them as they happen. Have you seen God as a patient Father who is helping you through the process?

We can step confidently into the day, knowing that we can change. "I have strength for all things in Christ who empowers me—I am ready for anything and equal to anything through him who infuses inner strength into me . . . [I am self-sufficient in Christ's sufficiency]" (Philippians 4:13 The Amplified Bible).

1. Lamberta Voget, *The Christian's Self-Prison* (Chicago, Ill.: Moody Press, 1960), p. 28, 29.

2. *Webster's New World Dictionary of the American Language*

3. Voget, *The Christian's Self-Prison*, p. 29.

LIVING
IN OUR
SECRET
PLACE

Every time you depend on Jesus Christ's love, you are abiding in him. "I am the true vine. . . . Abide in me." (John 15:1 and 4). For you are affirming that he lives in you to recreate rather than condemn. *Because he loves me, he will come to my rescue.* So you can trust him to help you over every rutted place and to act on your choice even though the process is painful.

My friend Ruth has learned how to live the abiding life. Her lower body is paralyzed and she is also inflicted with Raynoud's disease which causes veins to collapse, as well as Systemic Lupus, a malfunction of blood cells which causes an abundance of infection. Ruth still produces enough fruit to fill an orchard. She has strength of character, is unswerving in her faith, and is joyfully mischievious.

"I have an advantage," she told me. "I have to depend on God."

In a house fire when she was three months old, over 67 percent of her body was burned. Because her left brain was damaged as well, teachers classified her as retarded. But when she taught herself to read braille and to type, they changed their minds. Surgery strengthened her arms and legs; aids and glasses increased severely impaired hearing and vision. She was able to get around in a wheelchair and even drive a van.

By 1980, in spite of repeated hospitalizations, Ruth had earned four college degrees. "A fierce determination to make something of my life kept me going."

She was in college when she became a Christian, but even conversion couldn't make her believe that God could love someone as disfigured as she was. Then in 1972 during a weeklong seminar on the Bible, "God showed me in places like 1 John 3:1 that he really does love me. 'How great is the love the Father has lavished on us, that we should be called children of God!'

"It took months, but finally I was able to accept the love of God with all my heart. When that happened, I couldn't wait to tell others that he loves them, too, no matter what they're like."

Since then and in spite of continually deteriorating health and almost constant pain, she's been showing and telling God's love in her private counseling practice, her work with the mentally retarded, and as an advocate for the physically handicapped. She does it by counting moment by moment on Jesus Christ's life in her.

"He awakens me every morning with the measure of alertness and strength he knows I'll need for the day. A few Saturdays ago, I took part in a friend's wedding (despite twisted hands, she sewed her dress herself), then helped the rest of the day with a giant garage sale to benefit a quadruplegic alternative housing project.

"Twelve thirty that night I was awakened with an emergency phone call. My phone rang again at 4:00 A.M. with another emergency call. Four hours later I was still awake and alert in spite of the medication I'd taken. I knew God must have something for me. Sure enough, the phone rang. A friend's car had broken down and she needed my help. I got up and went to get her."

Those who visit Ruth come away awed. "But it's not me," she assures them. "It's my friend. He never fails me.

"Right now one of the things he's doing is helping me develop more patience—especially with Christians who aren't willing to help meet the needs of people around them."

WHAT ABIDING IS

Nine times in John chapter 15 Jesus used the word translated *abide* in the King James Bible. The same word is translated "stay (in a given state, relation or expectancy); continue, dwell . . . remain."[1] It's the word Lydia, a new convert, used years later when she invited Paul and his party to "stay at my house" and that Paul used when he instructed soldiers to "stay with the ship"

89

(Acts 16:15; 27:31). "After I am resurrected, stay in the same intimate relationship with me in your spirit that you have had while I was with you in the flesh on earth," Jesus was urging.

Kenneth S. Wuest adds that two of the New Testament meanings of *abide* are to "maintain unbroken fellowship with one . . . to be constantly present to help one."

He writes, "God is said to *meno* in Christ, i.e., to dwell as it were in Him, to be continually operative in Him by His divine influence and energy (John 14:10); Christians are said to *meno* in God, to be rooted as it were in Him, knit to Him by the Spirit they received from Him."[2]

To Annette, abiding in Christ is "establishing a daily relationship with God and by faith walking in that relationship. Saying, 'God, today I'll be filled with your Spirit and trust you to stop me when I do wrong.' I picture God as a circle and see myself walking in him that day. By faith I have to choose to believe I'm walking in the right way because I'm abiding in him."

Here is what he said on his way to Gethsemane about abiding in him: "I am the true vine and my Father is the gardener. He cuts off every branch in me that bears no fruit, while every branch that does bear fruit, he trims clean so that it will be even more fruitful. You are already clean because of the word I have spoken to you. Remain in me, and I will remain in you. No branch can bear fruit by itself: it must remain in the vine. Neither can you bear fruit unless you remain in me.

"I am the vine; you are the branches. If a man remains in me and I in him, he will bear much fruit; apart from me you can do nothing. If anyone does not remain in me, he is like a branch that is thrown away and withers; such branches are picked up, thrown into the fire and burned. If you remain in me and my words remain in you, ask whatever you wish, and it will be given you. This is to my Father's glory that you bear much fruit, showing yourselves to be my disciples" (John 15:1-8).

A PICTURE OF OUR RELATIONSHIP

Why did Jesus compare our relationship to him with a vine and its branches? Go look at one. If no vine is available in your immediate area, choose other vegetation like a tree or a plant. Vine, trunk, or stem—any of these pictorialize the living union that Jesus was talking about. I chose one in my backyard. Notice that—

1. It's alive.	1. In Christ we are alive.
2. The same sap flows through them.	2. Believers are one in Christ. His life flows through us.
3. A branch requires someone greater than itself to care for it.	3. We depend on our Gardener to do everything for our growth.
4. Its only purpose is to bear fruit.	4. Our purpose is to demonstrate God's qualities and do his work.
5. It must be pruned to produce fruit.	5. God has to remove old ways of thinking and behaving so we can demonstrate his life.
6. The more extensive the pruning, the greater the fruit.	6. The more we allow God to change us, the more fruitful we become.
7. Branches must remain disease free.	7. We must be free from sin to show God's life.
8. Branches must remain in the vine to bear fruit.	8. We must remain in intimacy with Jesus Christ to live as whole women.

We are as dependent on Christ as the branch is on the apple tree. The more complex our lives, the more we must depend on him to remain whole. "For in him we live and move and have our being" (Acts 17:28).

TO ABIDE IS TO STAY HOME

When I was growing up, home was a series of second and third-rate apartments. But I considered my real home to be Grandpa and Grandma's shingled farmhouse. Mother and I lived there together for a while, and I stayed there some summers, too.

The living room had bay windows where I could sit and cut out my paper dolls or look out at the orchard. Grandpa and I ate together at the big kitchen table, offering challenges, "I bet I can eat more clam chowder than you."

The tiny back bedroom was mine. I could lay in bed and listen to house sounds, to the woodpecker on the tree by the road, and curl up to sleep securely. I was in Grandpa's house, living in his love.

Even after we moved to Coney Island, I still thought of the farmhouse as my real home. In my memory I lived there—playing train under the dining room table with my cousin on Sunday afternoon while the big people talked.

I grew up, but part of me still wished for a place like that, where I always felt secure and loved. Fifteen years after I became a Christian, God showed me that I did have one—in my spirit, where he had come to live. I could go anywhere, experience any kind of trouble, and he'd be with me and I could be with him.

Jesus Christ in your spirit is your secret place. He is your real home.

Journal Exercise: What was your secret place? Perhaps it was an activity instead of a house. You felt most secure when you were being tucked in bed or coloring at the table while Mama cooked. Write about it. Tell how you felt. Then write a paragraph telling why Jesus is like that place. Describe one time recently when you found contentment during a crisis by abiding in him.

BRANCHES BEAR FRUIT

So long as we live in our secret place, we can demonstrate the nature of Christ himself—humility when we are misunderstood, joy over serving God, faith in the Father. We may be walking the floor in a ranch kitchen in Wyoming, feeling as dry in our souls as the acres outside our windows. But from within, from our reborn, indwelt spirits, we can still experience and generate peace.

True contentment doesn't come from having tailor-made lives. *If I only had married Jim, taken the other job, gone to college, stayed single, had children.* A sense of well-being and the ability to remain whole isn't for sale for $7.98 in the self-help section of our local bookstore.

It comes from living dependently in Christ and allowing him to demonstrate the same qualities through us that he did while he lived in Palestine. Make no mistake: we who are reborn do live in him now just as surely as we will live everlastingly in the golden city. Contentment comes from knowing we are united with Christ in our reborn spirits and are counting on that fact.

It is by counting on that fact that we bear fruit. "We all know what fruit is. The produce of the branch, by which men are refreshed and nourished. . . . A fruit-bearing tree lives not for itself, but wholly for those to whom its fruit brings refreshment and life. . . . As surely as a branch abiding in a fruitful vine bears fruit, so surely, yea, much more surely will a soul abiding in Christ with his fulness of blessing be made a blessing."[3]

The fruit we bear refreshes others. It is the qualities of God: love, joy, peace, patience, kindness, goodness, faith, gentleness, and self-control (Galatians 5:22 and 23). Fruit produces ministry. Instead of slamming the door behind when someone is spilling angry words at us because of a pressure-filled day, we can finally learn to say, "Stretch out on the sofa, and I'll massage your back."

Not one of my Grandpa's apple trees ate its own fruit. I ate it. So did Grandpa and Grandma and Uncle Stanley and Aunt Elizabeth and cousins Rhoda and Norman and other relatives and customers to whom Grandpa delivered it.

Our spiritual fruit is meant for our children, our husbands, our parents, brothers and sisters, co-workers and pew mates, the strangers next to us on the bus. We have love so we can be love.

WHAT DOES IT MEAN TO CHOOSE TO ABIDE?

For much of my Christian life I was frustrated by writers who told me that I should allow Christ to live his life through me, but never told me how. Or they made it sound easy. A whole-hearted surrender to God and I'd love those I'd hated and stand stalwart in situations I'd run from before.

But it's not that easy. No Christian wakes up on the morning after surrender and finds himself an everbearing branch bent low with clusters of patience and peace. Our surrender does, however, give God permission to make experiential the relationship spelled out on our adoption papers.

You are at the head of the day, anxious to abide in Christ. Already you've remembered that you've got a board meeting at nine. *God help me make my presentation without being nervous.*

You pull on jogging clothes and thump down the driveway and around the corner. The silhouette of a tall fir tree against the blue sky reminds you of God. *Your tree, Lord. You are Creator, and yet you live in me. That's amazing to think about but it's true.*

Back home as you shower, one of the kids pounds on the bathroom door. "Hey, Mom, hurry it up!" You want to yell back, "Get lost!" But you flash an inner look to God and are able to answer, "I'll be out in five minutes," without murder in your voice.

In the kitchen you discover that someone has spilled sugar on the floor and someone else has lost their math book and the bus is due in three minutes. You breathe "Help!" to God and crunch across the floor to get the broom and send one of the children to assist in the book search.

Every time you turn inwardly to the Vine, relate your moment to him, and depend on him to reflect life and godliness, you are living in him the way he commands. Abiding in Christ is just that: a commitment to live dependent on him and to choose moment by moment to put your commitment into practice.

ABIDING IS OBEYING

The more you choose to revel in God's love at every sharp corner of every day, the more natural it will be to obey him. Obedience is a love child. Because you love God, you trust him and want to obey.

I had been giving my love all of my life to myself. That self was doggedly determined that my love not ever be diverted to another. But now I was experiencing love from the one who originated it. As a result, I wanted to please him more than I wanted to please myself.

Neither fear nor duty nor responsibility to keep the law motivated me now, any more than it did when Jack and I exchanged vows. We loved, so instead of spending his extra money on himself, he bought me a rose each week. Rather than skip out Saturday mornings to be with his buddies, he stayed home and helped me clean our apartment. When I asked to have my pre-marriage dog move in with us (even though he wasn't anxious to be burdened with a pet in a New York city apartment), Jack agreed.

I learned to cook German spaetzles that he loved (even though to me they are still little globs of dough). To iron the dress shirts he wore to business. Every love act brought the giver as much reward as the recipient.

ABIDING AND PRAYER

To keep your relationship with Christ uppermost in your mind, you've learned that you need to meditate on his Word regularly. Through the day, you've been dialoging with him about his character, his love, and his will. Your prayers no longer sound like speeches with stilted, formal words. They are conversations between intimates.

You're having a running conversation with him about your day. "I know I should have whole wheat toast, but I sure want a jelly donut." "That woman on the stool next to me—she looks so miserable. What can I say to her?" "If I don't get some relief soon from these kids hanging on me every minute, I don't know what I'll do!" "Exercise, Lord? I keep starting out with all those good intentions . . ."

"I talk with God about everything," Ruth told me. "We talk about the music on the stereo and the dirty dishes in the sink." Prayer with words. Prayer without words that is a look in your spirit to God. Sighs, aches, inner smiles of thanks, bursts of joy, exclamations of reverential awe. From the jangle of the alarm to lights out.

Spiritual conversations like this will shape friendship between you. God's presence will become your experience. The more your inner woman abides in Christ, trusting him for the ability to deal with the situation at hand, the more you'll find that he is expressing himself through you the way he promised.

Journal Exercise: Whenever you find yourself in a tense situation, visualize yourself as a branch in the Vine and tell God you want to express his life. What feelings and attitudes hinder you? Ask God to prune you in these areas. What opportunities have you had to bear fruit?

Begin today to turn inwardly to the Vine during your mini-crises. Talk with him spontaneously about what matters to you. Record your experiences and ways you are discovering to deepen your vine/branch relationship and to bear fruit.

1. James Strong, *The Exhaustive Concordance of the Bible*, (Nashville: Abingdon Press, 1980).

2. Kenneth S. Wuest, "Studies in the Vocabulary of the Greek New Testament," Word Studies in the Greek New Testament, vol. 3, (Grand Rapids: Wm. B. Eerdmans Publishing Company, 1973), p. 64.

WOMEN
ARE
HUMAN,
TOO

To maintain an abiding relationship with Christ, attention to our personal well-being is absolutely essential. As branches, we are invaluable in the fruitbearing process. "Without the vine, the branch can do nothing . . . without the branch the vine can also do nothing."[1]

Humans get tired and simply cannot listen to one more account of "What he said to me and I said to him." We have to sleep, or we get short-tempered. We are not born knowing how to do anything except the things that keep us alive. We need to do our best to become healthy and hardy and remain that way.

A RESPONSIBILITY TO MAINTAIN OUR WELL-BEING

Yet some of us press ourselves to give when we should be out for repair. Perhaps we do it because we still don't really believe in our worth or because our personal sense of individuality is fuzzy. Our identities have become tangled with those of our husbands or mothers. Our value depends on who we are to them today and on their current wholeness, instead of our own.

Some women are like I was—unsure and unable to listen, discern, and decide for themselves. Every respected evangelical pastor or teacher or writer is their authority.

Because their concept of submission is off balance, they feel as though they have no right to maintain their personal well-being—to develop their minds, feed their souls, care for their bodies, or cultivate their talents.

God did not create women to give themselves totally away—to be branches doling out chunks of themselves until there's nothing left. We are to give out from ourselves—out from the life of Christ within us. "The daily inflowing of the life-sap of the Holy Spirit is his only power to bring forth fruit."[2]

Even when we women do begin to believe that we are valuable branches and that we must nurture ourselves so we can be Christ to others, we groan that we haven't time.

There is always something more to be done. Over 60 percent of us hold down jobs in addition to our roles as homemakers. But usually it isn't that we can't make an hour for ourselves occasionally. It's the feeling that "we ought to be doing something more, different, or better."[3] *I should give this hour to my husband, my children, the church.*

Unconsciously, we have written a syllogism and instructed ourselves to live by it:

Today's women are accomplishing more.

I am one of today's women.

l should be accomplishing more.

We have our own built-in concept of what a woman, wife, and mother should be. She is the Proverbs 31 ideal paraded before us every Mother's Day—with Hannah and Sarah and echoes of our own personal female role models thrown in.

But "superwomen exist only in TV commercials: real women must set priorities and decide where—and when—to concentrate their energies."[4] And some of it had better be on ourselves.

WAYS TO STAY HEALTHY BRANCHES

Gloria is a wife, mother of three preschool children, and works part-time besides. She was continually frustrated because she had no time for herself. "No matter what I do—from talking on the phone to cleaning the toilets—the kids are always there clamoring for attention.

"Finally, I realized that I simply had to get time away from my responsibilities at home, because I wasn't up to what I wanted to be emotionally. That's when I started hiring a baby sitter one morning a week. It had to be fitted into the budget, of course. But it really helps to know that those blocks of hours are mine.

"All week, I look forward to that morning. For a while, I spent the time at the library. The first time I sat there and looked around and listened to all that quiet, I thought, "Boy, this has got to be illegal, immoral, or fattening."

When Evelyn's children were small, she chose to stay home with them. "I'm glad I did. But everything I was involved in was pragmatic—even decorating the house. When I was younger, I'd done a lot of drawing. Things like that were a part of myself that had disappeared.

"Not only that, but nothing was ever done, ever under control. And I seem to need a lot of time by myself, and I didn't have it.

"It seemed as though I'd made a box and put myself in it. Finally, I had a talk with my pastor and he said I needed to get out of the house one day a week. I hadn't had enough good feelings about myself to give myself permission to do that. But when I did, it helped tremendously."

When I begin to feel wrung dry despite the fact that I have been communicating with God and meditating on his Word, I know I need time to be Marion for awhile. "When one is a stranger to oneself, then one is estranged from others too."[5] Sometimes, I find myself by being with a friend, other times by being alone.

At different times in our lives, the things we need to do to maintain a sense of ourselves changes. When our children toddle after us even refusing to let us go to the bathroom alone, we ache for solitude or for the company of someone over four. Or we are fed up with loose ends because our housework is never done and our "Still to do" list is always longer than the items crossed off. We simply must finish something. For Gloria, that's a craft project. "Something I can hold up and say, 'See what I made?'"

Women who are alone a lot need to integrate into society again. Sometimes I go to town to run a few errands and then sit and eat an ice cream cone and watch people pass. Satisfied to see other versions of myself, I go home assured again that I am part of a whole.

This year I have scheduled Bible study and breakfast with two friends each week. For an hour or so, we talk about the kinds of branches we are and the kinds we are struggling to become. Voluntarily, we have made ourselves accountable to one another to persist in becoming whole.

Another woman I know takes mini-retreats. She may climb in her car and drive to a park where she sets up a lawn lounge and settles for a few hours with a thermos of tea, her Bible, and her God. Sometimes she simply unplugs the phone and goes into her bedroom, taking her journal or a book she's wanted to read and relaxes, stopping occasionally to hear neighborhood sounds for the first time in weeks.

A young mother who works as a consultant travels to twenty-two different places of business. Eventually she says she falls apart. "But now when that happens, my husband takes over. He learned how hard it is to fill dual roles earlier in our marriage when he agreed to take more responsibility at home.

"He knows that when I'm fragmented I don't have anything left for him. So he fixes me a bath complete with towels and candles and tells me 'Lock yourself in and don't come out until you're ready.'"

The God who was able to bring order out of Genesis 1 is able to show us ways to remain whole branches Monday through Friday at six o'clock. But if he's going to do that for us, we must keep living at home in Jesus Christ and assume the responsibility to do the things he shows us.

He will not push us to spend regular time in intimate communion with him, to plan for solitude just to think and be, to get more sleep, to eat yogurt instead of coffeecake. We must take the initiative ourselves.

Journal Exercise: Do you have trouble taking time for yourself? Why? Write about ways you might spend two hours each week set aside for yourself. Budget that time. Write about how it changes your perspective.

CULTIVATING SELF-DISCIPLINE

Instead of taking the responsibility ourselves to do the things that will make us healthy branches, we often shift the blame for our condition. *If only my husband would insist that I rest after work or take an evening out with the girls. If only he would diet with me (or exercise or study the Bible or pray or switch to natural foods).*

Other people's support can keep us afloat when we're floundering, but no one can practice self-discipline for me but me. And I learn self-discipline by making a series of small, daily choices to obey the Scripture and the Holy Spirit. *Temperance:* bed at eleven instead of one more TV show. *Good temple management:* herb tea instead of one more cup of coffee.

But sometimes we want the coffee or the quiet hours alone with the TV, even though we have to be up at six. If we are to become Jesus women, we must learn to agree humbly with God and accept his forgiveness every time we do follow sin's crooked finger. Other times when we feel guilty, however, it may not be for a valid reason. We must learn the difference between real and false guilt.

REAL GUILT AND FALSE GUILT

Heavy with false guilt, I shuffled through months after my husband and I resigned from rural missionary work. Ego insisted I had deserted God's cause, so I felt guilty about everything from the way I did my housework to the way I studied the Bible. Only later, after the trauma was over, was I able to understand what had happened and distinguish between missing God's mark and the trembling of a wounded psyche.

I smile a lot more because now I know the difference between being sinful and being human. We are acting sinfully when we disobey a principle outlined in God's written revelation. We are acting humanly when we act according to the limitations imposed on homo sapiens.

HUMANNESS AND SINFULNESS

It is not sinful to be human, but humans are sinful. The world that God created is not evil, but evil is present in the world, and every part of it has been corrupted. It is not sinful to be tired and need a rest, but mothers who are tired and do not rest are not able to hand out clusters of patient understanding. Neither are ones who suppose they must do everything that needs to be done, or who suppress their feelings "because good Christians don't get mad."

Because the world is twisted out of shape, we become ill. One of my closest friends has been a semi-invalid for about two years with a tough-to-treat illness. Her physiological problems triggered depression. On my visits, we talk about the fact that she is not ill because she has sinned, but because she lives in a world in which the roses in her yard get black spot, her lettuce is eaten by slugs, and humans contract disease.

Women like her find that some days joy is buried beneath the symptoms of their illness. They come to understand this is normal for humans and stop condemning themselves. They recover not by pretending perfection, but by owning the humanness that relates us all and abiding by faith in the Divine One.

Journal Exercise: Have you been failing to take into consideration that, although you are a Christian, you are also a human being? How has that evidenced itself in your daily life? Have you denied that you have human emotions? Overextended yourself? Expected perfection? What steps can you take to change that?

COPING WITH OUR PHYSIOLOGY

Not only are we human branches, but we are female human branches, each with our own peculiar hormonal cycles. It took years before I realized that the monthly tenseness I was experiencing was from premenstrual syndrome, not spiritual malaise. To greater or lesser degrees about 60 percent of us are afflicted with bloating, edginess, anxiety, nausea, headaches, insomnia, depression, and a variety of other symptoms during the days before menstruation and some during ovulation as well.

The cycle which allows us to become pregnant and have babies can also cause us to stumble into another gully, postpartum depression. "During the last three months of pregnancy, your body is literally flooded with hormones. These hormones make you relaxed and complacent . . . within hours of childbirth, however, these hormones taper off a dramatic 40 percent . . . the ecstasy you may feel during late pregnancy and childbirth can be replaced by anger and deep sadness and fear."[6] A friend told me, "When postpartum depression hit me, I felt guilty because I was unappreciative of this baby God had given me."

Women have to cope with their peculiar physiology most of their lives. When ovulation finally ends and menopause begins, so do hot flushes, night sweats, and sometimes insomnia, nervousness, and various levels of depression. When menopause hit me, I often awoke about 2:00 A.M. and stared into the dark until 4:00 or so.

I prayed for God to heal me. He did not. Instead, he taught me to worship him when I lay awake, and to rest in him, and when I did, the hours changed color. That's when I realized God wasn't going to pull a miracle out of his God bag like an indulgent parent and take all the hurts out of life for me.

I stopped worrying that he loved me less than I thought he did, or that I had sinned or didn't have enough faith. I looked and listened for wisdom to know what I could do to sleep better, and he showed me that I should relax before bedtime and pare down my schedule and get hormones from my doctor.

I was growing up. Menses, their side effects and cessation, pregnancy and the months after, physiological malfunctions, human emotions, attitudes, and limitations are part of what it means to be woman. They are not spiritual problems, but God will help me through them and comfort me along the way. My eating and exercise habits, my hormone and blood sugar level, and my emotions all contribute to the way I feel. And the way I feel contributes to the way I mature.

When the bunions on my big toes ache, I can hate a world that forced me to wear the too short, cheap shoes that triggered their development. Or I can cut holes in the sides of my tennis shoes (the way my doctor suggested) and wear them at home to get relief. And when someone comes to the door and catches me with my ugly, crooked toes sticking out, I can move into Christ, laugh at myself, and bear fruit.

Menopausal insomnia or aching bunions—they can turn me into a temporarily barren branch or bind me more closely to Christ and teach me more about spirituality.

1. Andrew Murray, *Abide in Christ* (Ft. Washington, Pa.: Christian Literature Crusade, new edition, 1968), p. 28.

2. Ibid.

3. Susan Jacoby, "In Praise of Imperfect Women," *Woman's Day* 24 November 1981, p.66.

4. Ibid, p. 73.

5. Anne Morrow Lindbergh, *Gift from the Sea* (New York: Vintage Books, 1955), p. 44.

6. Diane Lynch-Fraser, *The Complete Postpartum Guide*(New York: Harper & Row, 1978), p. 16.

FROM
GETTING
TO
GIVING

Once a woman has begun to learn to live at home in Jesus Christ, she is ready to put on the roles and relationships she laid aside and wear them well. For now she will not have to use daughter, wife, mother, and secretary to give her a sense of identity and acceptance.

Layering roles and relationships over one another—clerk over daughter, wife over clerk, mother over wife—will not create a person any more than skirts and blouses and vests and sweaters and jackets will. (When a role and relationship no longer exist—we lose our job or our husband—who are we?)

But I had been trained to think differently. Before I could print my name, I lisped what I wanted to be when I grew up. "A nurse," I said as I took Bear's temperature. "And a Mama, too."

It took me years to realize I'd been answering the wrong question. It's not "What will I be when I grow up?" but "Who will I be?" Which of all my relationships will determine who I am?

The answer, of course, is my eternal relationship with God. Centered on him, with his Spirit filling my spirit and energizing my mind, emotions, and will, I experience personal integration. My reborn, indwelt spirit becomes the control tower of my life. As I live in him and he lives in me, I am complete.

FREE FROM PREOCCUPATION WITH OURSELVES

Human relationships do fulfill us, but expecting them to always do so has been disappointing. Today they succeed; tomorrow, they fail. Children who squeeze us hard or take us by the hand to "show us somepin'" may act as strangers when they reach adulthood. Our parents may bring us gifts, but they stay to set us straight. Safer to hold them a length away, just in case they intend to kick instead of kiss.

But now human rebuffs need no longer kick holes

in our soul. God is the keeper of our ego. Because we are learning that he values us and that we can live trusting his love, we are more willing to be vulnerable before others. We are growing free of preoccupation with ourselves. (What does he think of me? What if I make a mistake?)

God accepts me as I am and is helping me grow more mature. I no longer need to spend my time projecting a slicked-up image. I can give my attention instead to the people in my life—to hug them to me and give without guarantee that I'll receive, just as the Father asks. "Dear friends, since God so loved us, we also ought to love one another" (1 John 4:11).

Experiencing God's kindness . . . we can be kind to others, whether or not they have been kind to us.

Forgiven . . . we can forgive others even though they are likely to hurt us again. And again.

A friend of God . . . we can be friends to others, demonstrating caring for them consistently the way God does for us.

Lavished with God's love . . . we can lavish his love on others—even in the ways most hard for us to do.

Accepted . . . we can accept others. Their criticism need not wound the way it once did.

Our needs met . . . we can meet others' needs, empathizing, asking ourselves, "If I were them, what would I want?"

TWO KINDS OF RELATIONSHIPS

Human relationships are simply connections to others. They can be divided into two groups. The first are those with whom we have long-term relationships. This group includes parents, husband, fiancée, children, grandchildren, extended family, employer, employee, Christians with whom we fellowship.

Modular relationships are the second type. Alvin Toffler says, "Rather than entangling ourselves with the whole man, we plug into a module of his personality."[1] These modules include salespersons, acquaintances, those we see only in church on Sunday morning or at the club once a month or on the bus riding home from work. They also includes those who perform services for us, like doctors and dentists.

EXPERIENCING FREEDOM IN OUR RELATIONSHIPS

Now that we see ourselves as God sees us and are allowing our union with God to define who we are, we can live out of that union in our relationships with other people. Then those relationships become extensions of the one we have with God.

As parents, we can stop craving our children's approval. Now we know that our self-worth doesn't depend on our child's perception of us, so we can say "no" without crumbling. We can give our attention to building up their sense of adequacy . . . allow them to develop their individuality.

As wives, instead of criticizing our husbands, we can accept them as they are and act toward them in love, even when they are too preoccupied or frustrated to give love back.

As job holders, we can extend our friendship. "I began to see how important it was to risk rejection by others in the office and to build personal relationships with them. When I did, God gave me opportunities to minister his love."

As in-laws, we can do what a friend of mine did. "I kept trying to make an impression on my mother-in-law, to prove I was good enough for her son. I know now that it's okay just to be me."

As Christians, we may have been living in carefully constructed, safe compartments, closed in from one another. On committees, we serve polite conversation like canapés. For me, change meant letting my Christian friends know that I was human —that I got discouraged, harbored resentments just like they did.

LIVING BEFORE GOD ALONE

The people closest to us are often the ones who cause us the most pleasure—and the most pain. Their misshapen egos may have been the ones that rubbed against our own so that we came away raw and bleeding. "Irregular people," Joyce Landorf calls them.

They may be parents who failed to nourish us because they didn't know how or in-laws whose worth is tied up in a son they can't afford to give up. Our brothers and sisters may refuse closeness because they still remember the shame of comparison with us or of favoritism by a parent.

We may have spent too many years expecting intimacy they could not give. God may not be able to change them—at least not right away—but he can change the way we see and respond to them. Instead of mourning the inadequacy of their love for us, we can be "filled to the measure of all the fullness of God" (Ephesians 3:19). Satisfied, we'll be better able to take them as they are.

Claire grew up trying to win her mother's approval. "Once when I was a teenager, I fixed my hair in a style my mother disapproved of. She wouldn't speak to me for days. Finally, I changed it back so our relationship would be normal again.

"A Bible seminar I went to after I was an adult helped me see that it wouldn't make any difference what I did. I couldn't change my mother. What is important is my relationship with God. Everyone has expectations for us: we can't fulfill them all. We need to line them up with his expectations of us and let the rest fall by the wayside. What he wants is for me to keep showing my love and concern for her."

For years Jenny tried to be the daughter she

115

thought her mother wanted her to be. "I scrubbed my house clean because I knew she'd look when she came to visit. Everything had to look the way I thought my mother wanted it.

"I transferred those feelings to my husband, too. I tried and tried to be the wife and mother he wanted—to do everything right. But it wasn't him who cared. It was me.

"It was painful to realize that no matter what I did do, I wasn't going to gain my mother's approval. That was painful, but a big turning point in my life. It took time to realize I could be the person I am.

The guilt is gone, I can feel good about myself even when I don't accomplish a task to the level of competence I desire. I still like a clean house, but it's not a compulsive thing now." Jenny has learned to accept her mother as she is, not as she'd like her to be, and to relate to her within the restrictions of her mother's personality.

Journal Exercise: List the people with whom you have long-term relationships. Next to each, write the changes you'd like to make in the way you behave toward them. Choose one, and look for little ways you can begin to effect that change. Record your experiences. Then go on to do the same in another relationship.

THE FUNCTIONS OF OUR RELATIONSHIPS WILL CHANGE

Out of each of these long-term relationships grows a set of responsibilities. Sometimes, we call these "roles." They exist for all of us. Mothers must scrub strained spinach off the high chair tray and walk the floor from four to midnight because the baby has colic. Supermarket cashiers must punch the keys and say "Have a nice day."

Roles differ for each of us. We may each be wives, but some of us are responsible to type our husband's letters and keep his books, while others must iron his underwear.

The functions we perform for those in our lives change as the stages of our lives change. We used to pack our children's lunches; now we send cookies to their college dorm. We used to baby-sit our brother; now we help him write his résumé.

No longer do we need to use work to prove worth. We know now that we have worth. So we are free to wash clothes, dishes, floors, walls, toilets, and the guppy bowl because we are in love with God, not to get love from others. Not to show Mama or even ourselves that we are capable. Each act can become an expression of God's love in me for the people in my life.

Since we do tend to lapse back into old ways, particularly under stress, we'll want to check ourselves periodically. Am I doing too much for my children so they'll keep needing me? Am I pushing myself to get the housework done or keeping my appointment book full because I think that accomplishment equals approval?

Am I trying to live up to others' unrealistic expectations—calling mother twice a day because she expects it; getting dinner on the table by six because my family expects it, even though I don't get home until after five?

Have I given up and put an invisible sign over my life that reads "Bless this mess" because I feel completely unable to do what I need to do?

Journal Exercise: List your long-term relationships and the roles each requires. For example, because I am Jack's wife, I wash his clothes, cook his meals, etc. Ask yourself: How many of these roles am I performing to prove my worth? What changes would I like to make so I'll be doing jobs to demonstrate love? Take small steps to effect these changes.

GIVING TO ACQUAINTANCES

The more we live in love with God, the more we'll want to let him turn modular relationships into real ones, too. Instead of staring at the salesclerk who rings up our groceries every week as though he is invisible, we'll take notice of him. When it seems appropriate we'll ask, "How's it going?"

My husband Jack has taught me the most about how to relate to people I see often but don't really know. "Look at those fingers fly on the keys," he'll comment to a fast clerk. "How long did it take you to get that way?"

He knows that the girl who pours his coffee is working two jobs and the man who pumps his gas is alone now because his wife walked out on him. Because I've worked as a salesclerk myself, I know how important these exchanges can be. They're natural for Jack, but not for me. I have to focus on Christ in me so I'll remember to treat the clerk who cashes my checks at the drive-up window as a friend, instead of just plugging in to her banker module.

I am motivated to act when I realize that Jesus didn't see the Samaritan woman at the well simply as someone who gave him a drink. Nor was he ever too preoccupied maintaining his image as the son of God to establish relationships with this group of people.

Journal Exercise: List your primary modular relationships. This week, begin with one and cultivate their friendship in whatever ways seem appropriate. Record the results.

KINDNESS AS A LIFE STYLE

In addition, people with whom we have no relationship at all pass through our lives. I knew that I was becoming more secure about my identity in Christ when I began initiating casual conversation with women like these whom I didn't know. Strangers had always been the hardest of all for me to build a relationship with. *Unimportant*, my old mind insisted. *What good is a two-minute conversation?*

Still, occasionally, God prompted. *Smile. Say*

thanks. Talk about how cold/hot/windy it is. About her baby/puppy/hand knit sweater.

Finally, I understood why it was important to obey. I was offering a touch of friendship in a society alienated from one another. God was training me to see others.

There were dozens of strangers in my world every week. They'd been there all along, of course, but I hadn't really been seeing them. I was too busy staring inside myself.

The more I noticed the people in line with me at the supermarket and smiled at them, the more I spoke to the woman waiting next to me for a bus, the more I was training myself to see others and their needs and to leave myself and my own needs with God.

Slowly (and often painfully), I was becoming free of egocentricity so that I could relate to others with the hope of meeting their needs rather than my own. I was free to build in them a biblical sense of self, the way God had been doing for me.

1. Alvin Toffler, *Future Shock* (New York: Bantam Books, 1970), p. 97.

OUR
CRISIS
CENTER

I nevitably, we all experience the trauma of crisis. It may come suddenly when we get a phone call. "Harry had a heart attack. It looks bad." Other times, it happens because some longstanding problem has exploded in our faces. For Helen and her husband, that problem was a business struggling to survive.

Finally, they had to go through bankruptcy. "I was firmly against it," Helen told me. "I was afraid it would ruin our Christian testimony. I was afraid of what people would think.

"But there comes a point when you have to put the whole thing in God's hands and ask him to guide. We felt after praying and thinking that there was nothing else to do.

"When the business folded, I was torn apart. I couldn't even pray. I didn't doubt God, but at times I didn't read my Bible or go to church, mostly because I was so emotional I couldn't hold myself together."

For my mother, the crisis took place when my father became mentally ill. *How will Marion and I survive? I'm too sick and my husband can't support us.*

I knew that Mama was at an impasse when she sat rocking and reading her Bible, never smiling in my direction, only staring off at scenes I couldn't see.

Twenty years later, I was doing the same thing. I even had her Bible. I experienced the same anxiety. *Only a few dollars left in our bank account. When that's gone, then what?*

I felt guilty because I couldn't trust God and because I was afraid our financial situation was my fault—punishment, maybe, for some sin. I was anxious and too ashamed of my anxiety to tell anyone.

CRISIS CAN BE A TURNING POINT IN FAITH

Like most others in crisis, I became fragmented. My mind cranked out melodramas in which my family and I had been evicted and had to turn to charity the way

Mama had to do. Although I wanted to, I simply couldn't trust God and live so that the Holy Spirit was in control of all of me. Instead, every part of me seemed to be functioning on its own.

Over and over, God brought me back to Hebrews 12:12 and 13. "So, lift up your drooping hands and strengthen your shaky knees; step out straight ahead with your feet, so that which is lame may not be dislocated but rather be healed" (MLB).

The more I chose to obey that command even though what I really wanted was to run into the bedroom and cry, the more that crisis became a turning point toward faith. I know now that's how God means to use the crucial situations that barge into our lives.

Jesus' words telling us how to do that were spoken to Christians in crisis. Their master was on his way to Calvary. He was put to death on a Roman cross instead of being crowned King of Israel. Fear crowded out their faith. The historical dilemma has been how to take his words "Trust in God, trust also in me" from the page to our pain (John 14:1).

QUESTIONS ARISE FROM CRISIS

Like the eleven, we want to know "Why?" Not knowing why is perhaps worst of all. *What have I done? Is God different from what I've believed?*

Evelyn agonized over questions like these when her son was burned. She kept asking herself if God had allowed it to happen because she was so stubborn he had to use something like that to get to her. She was a long time sorting things out.

"One of the things I learned was that I was afraid of God. I never would have imagined that was so. And deep down, I thought if you did things right your life would go right. The basic conclusion I came to as to why my son was burned is that we live in a sinful world. There are lots of reasons why things like this happen."

123

When Gloria had one miscarriage and then a second, she became angry with God. "Some people who haven't gone through that don't realize that the baby is a very real person to the mother—one with whom she's deeply in love."

Over and over she kept storming to herself, "Look at all these women who have endless abortions, and I want a baby and can't have one!"

Going through a divorce when she was young and had no family or church to lean on left Elaine feeling completely fragmented. "When it was over, I couldn't believe I'd survive. But afterwards, I was hurt, suicidal, and sick a lot."

We shatter, not only because our basic concept of what life is supposed to be like is challenged, but also because our basic human needs—to have physical, economic, and emotional safety; to be loved, recognized, and respected; to belong; to be seen as worthwhile and capable—are threatened. So we rise on our haunches, stiffened, with our ears cocked. Alarm "is followed by the stage of resistance. . . . We hide our emotions . . . try to solve our problem 'through inner change.' When this is not effective we dispose of the problem by burying it—or think that we do."[1]

One of the most traumatic times for a middle-aged woman I talked with was when her last child left home. Another said, "My husband retired two years ago. It's been one of the hardest times of my life."

Others experience shattered illusions when Christians take on more human dimensions than divine. For some, the crisis is illness. "I thought I had the world by the tail," Harriet said. "Then I got sick and stayed that way. I couldn't do any of the things I used to do. My illness led to depression. I felt worthless."

Ingrained is the idea that we Christians should be able to face any number of dilemmas undaunted—chin held high, shoulders squared, soul under control. No shaking or quaking or midnight tears. When we find out that we can't, we're ashamed.

JESUS IS TO BE OUR EXAMPLE

Jesus Christ didn't respond that way. He anguished in Gethsemane at the crisis of the cross until his sweat was as great drops of blood. Divinity wore humanity—nervous system, adrenal glands, and all.

But he knew what to do in crisis. Luke 22:39-42 says that just before the soldiers came to arrest him, Jesus went to the Father in prayer. Unashamedly, he showed his father his pain and counted on what he knew was true. "My Father ... is greater than all" (John 10:29).

Jesus recognized his father's sovereignty over the situation and knew that, through union with him, he could overcome his human nature. "Yet not my will, but yours be done" (Luke 22:42).

Because Jesus kneeled at his own turning point and won, he can help us through ours. So follow hard after him. For the sons of Adam, like the second Adam, the time to kneel is when the sound of the ax first echoes through our forest.

Like Christ, our words may be for deliverance. David's often were. The Psalms show that.

He was completely honest with God about the way he felt. "I am in distress; my eyes grow weak with sorrow, my soul and my body with grief" (Psalm 31:9). No pretense to be "Fine, thank you."

STRENGTH CAN BE GLEANED FROM SCRIPTURE

As soon as we are able, we must absorb truth on which to stand from Scripture.

After her miscarriage Gloria's Dad studied Habbakuk with her. "So many verses said that faith is believing God when you don't understand.

"In the end of the book, Habakkuk realized the

city was going to be destroyed. He said 'Though the fig tree does not bud and there are no grapes on the vines, though the olive crop fails and the fields produce no food, though there are no sheep in the pen and no cattle in the stalls, yet I will rejoice in the Lord, I will be joyful in God my Savior' (3:17 and 18). It helped me to be able to say, 'God, even though I don't understand, I know you're still in control of this situation.'" Her parents' accepting her while she struggled played a significant part, too.

After you have shown God your anxiety and meditated on Scripture, sit quietly before him in worship and submission. Praise may only be a faint inner warmth at first, but gradually God will enable you to trust the truth again. Inner integration into Christ will start to take place.

Anxiety will return to lap at your feet. Even Jesus' human responses in crisis didn't end in Gethsemane. At the ninth hour on the cross, he cried in a loud voice. "My God, my God, why have you forsaken me?" (Matthew 27:46). Unashamed, we can pray our psalms of distress and let God turn our minds back toward hope. Helen said, "It took time, but now I have an assurance that the Lord is with me and I am abiding in him."

Journal Exercise: Review one time you faced a major crisis. What things did you do that were constructive and helped you trust God? What things did you do that increased your anxiety? What changes would you make?

KEEP MINI-CRISES IN PERSPECTIVE

In addition to these major crises, our way Home is pocked with mini-crises as well. They begin before our eyes are fully open and we realize that we have no bread for lunches. Someone pours cereal on the floor instead of in the bowl. The cat wants in and the dog wants out. The phone rings and the baby is screaming.

Women say:

"The time when I walk in the door after work is the worst. It's a matter of who's going to scream loudest and get my attention first."

"As a single parent, my life is full of mini-crises. I have to do everything myself, and there are always too many things to do. I have to crowd things in and chaos is the result."

"Working in my husband's business causes lots of daily crises. When I remind him of something, sometimes it sounds like nagging."

"I have three small children. They have so many needs that my feelings build up and I scream at them. Then I lay a guilt trip on myself. *What a lousy mother you are!*"

The fuss with the neighbor, the flat tire on the way to work—both can be opportunities to cultivate a strong, inner woman. Choose to turn to Christ within and smile across the fence and speak peace (even though your neighbor has griped about the tree limb hanging over on her side of the fence).

So long as we take the eternal view, our mini-crises remain in perspective. I first understood about keeping things in perspective when I was drinking coffee at an Oregon coast restaurant one weekday morning. Directly in front of me out the window was scattered debris and lumber from construction. But beyond was the ocean, blue stretched to the horizon.

Trash and beauty were both part of the same scene. So it is in my life. While ants trail up the kitchen wall (because it's autumn and cold and wet and they want in), God Almighty is with me. Both the crisis and the Christ are present realities. The way I respond to the first is determined by how sure I am of the second.

Journal Exercise: What mini-crises reoccur most regularly in your life? Why? What can you do to reduce their frequency? To keep from becoming fragmented? Pray about your responses and practice ways God shows you to change. Write about the results.

Through Christ, we are in control. My friend Donna knew that when she went into the operating room for cancer in her lower bowel. When she awoke, she would have a permanent colostomy.

"I wasn't afraid," she told me later. "God had already prepared me by leading me to think through what I'd do if I ever got cancer. I decided that I'd commit myself to him and trust him to do whatever was his will in the situation.

"When it did happen, I made that commitment." It helped that cancer was not the first crisis in Donna's life. Earlier, her husband had a drinking problem and she had learned then to live in Jesus Christ and trust him for wisdom for herself and a changed life for her husband. The Lord accomplished both.

After she recuperated and learned to adjust to life with a colostomy, she began to minister to new ostomy patients and women with cancer. Because she'd been where they were, she knew what to say.

She's had cancerous growths removed twice more, and underwent extensive radiation treatments the second time. But her spiritual woman has remained whole.

I still have the note she wrote me on the evening before her first surgery in 1975. "Am about to embark on a new venture of faith! I am looking forward to what the Lord will bring out of it for his glory, and what he will teach me through it." The other day when I reread it, I thought of Jesus "Who for the joy set before him endured the cross, scorning its shame, and sat down at the right hand of the throne of God.

"Consider him . . . so that you will not grow weary and lose heart" (Hebrews 12:2 and 3).

1. Walter McQuade and Ann Aikman, *Stress* (New York: E.P. Dutton & Co., Inc.), p.16.

**BECOMING
COMPLETE**

I know now that Mama was not the sum of her roles and relationships—Isadore's wife, Stanley's sister, Grandpa's daughter, the English woman's friend. I came to see that when I realized my own identity did not reside in who I am to others or what I do.

We are both persons—she, Florence Maria Peterson Siegel and I, Marion Anna Siegel Duckworth. She wore housedresses to bed and I wear a long, pink nightgown. But the real women are the individuals beneath our skin.

Our mothers will always be Mama to us, of course. But when we are finally able to look beyond that relationship and see and accept them as individuals, we will allow them to model for us in the most important way of all.

For then we will see them as human beings who struggled to become whole the way we have—sometimes gaining, sometimes losing. They had different social environments as well as different backgrounds, personalities, and experiences with which to contend. Where they failed, we can sympathize, for we, too, fail. Where they succeed, we can emulate and be thankful.

The person beneath my Mama's skin became alive in a country Methodist church where she found God. Through illnesses and poverty and loneliness, that inner spiritual woman took on strength and substance. Now that I see her with adult eyes, I know what I could not have known then—that beneath her steady calmness was a melee between flesh and spirit, fear, and faith. We have that in common, too.

GROWING TOWARD THE GOAL

It's my turn now to press on toward the goal. More than anything, I want my inner woman to grow strong. It has been comforting to know that our struggles are alike. By giving Mama permission to be human and to fail, I have given myself permission to do so as well. Even her mistakes can be a legacy to me, because I can learn from them.

I want to grow strong, not hard. A few years ago, I learned the difference when I saw again a Christian woman I know. "She's changed," I thought. It took months for me to understand how.

Instead of allowing the trouble through which she'd gone to make her strong, she'd let it harden her. Strength is "power that resists destruction;" hardness is "unyieldedness to the touch. Not easily dented."[1] My friend had steeled herself so she wouldn't feel more pain. But in the process she'd become imprisoned inside her own fortress.

I understood because there have been times when I ve decided to "tough it" myself. But before long, I found myself becoming thick-skinned. So I chose to live as a branch again. And discovered that healthy branches are vulnerable, but they are also resilient. They may be wounded but, because of Life in them, they are not destroyed. Strength is at their core.

WHOLENESS FOUND IN CHRIST

Women who live as branches united with the Vine and are freed from false ideas that they are valueless or alone have the ability to realize their potential through the life of Christ within. They are the ones who can become fulfilled. This kind of fulfillment isn't the "have it all" fixation by which the word is currently defined. Career, bank account, car, luxurious vacation, marriage, home, family—satisfying avocation wrested from an unwilling world through daily hand-to-hand combat.

It is completeness. The Holy Spirit is the overseer of the honing of every facet of our personhood into the likeness of Christ. This includes the way we use our intellect, express ourselves emotionally, make decisions, project our personality, employ our abilities, and present our selves to the world. Under his tutelage, these selves are integrated into one whole woman "filled to the measure of all the fullness of God" (Ephesians 3:19).

Paul advises how we can arrive at that place. "He may strengthen you with power through his Spirit in your inner being, so that Christ may dwell in your hearts through faith" (Ephesians 3:16 and 17). Cultivating Christ's "at-home-ness" Kenneth S. Wuest calls it. The Savior has been present in our lives, but if we persist in abiding in him, he can "finally settle down and feel completely at home,"[2] assured that he can express himself through any aspect of our personhood.

That is wholeness.

WOMEN WHO ARE BECOMING

For me the process of cultivating my potential began when I understood my true identity as a cherished daughter of the Eternal God. The years before, I groped in the dark, feeling blindly for clues. *But I love you, Marion*, put me on track.

Like every other woman, I was created to be a unique child in the family. God would help me express my individuality and capabilities, shaping them in the family image. Only he knows me completely, only he can shape me.

Like me, Elaine has begun to think of herself these last few years as someone who is evolving. No longer does she identify herself in terms of work. "My talents may not be real clear yet, but there's something more to me than being Charlie's mother or Frank's wife. I'm in the process of discovering who that person is and feeling better about myself as I do."

CULTIVATING OUR INTELLECT

One of the most important ways we can cultivate our potential is to learn to think for ourselves. Helen told me, "Since I learned to like myself, I've discovered that I can have my own thoughts about things." That's what I've been learning this past decade of seeing myself biblically—to know what I think. It's been a new experience, because for years I doubted my ability to reason out issues based on my understanding of truth. I didn't trust my conclusions.

I know now that God created women as rational beings. Married or not, they are responsible to cultivate and utilize their intelligence. So, we women must learn to think deeply and broadly. Knowing the current refunding deals and which brand of disposable diapers are best is not enough. We must think for ourselves about what it means to be separated from the world, about the right to die, and the sanctity of life. By knowing what we think under God, we can exert influence in our segment of a largely humanistic society.

King Lemuel's proverbial woman who spoke "with wisdom and faithful instruction" knew that she had cultivated her intellectual abilities so that "her husband has full confidence in her" (Proverbs 31:11 and 26). She was no ancient prototype of a Christian wife steeped in nonthink. She combined knowledge with wisdom.

It was easier for me to understand how I could cultivate my intellect than to allow Christ to be at home in my emotional nature. Fear and uncertainty had been my reflexive responses for too long. Like thick autumn fog, they enveloped my days and obscured my perceptions.

Living in the presence of God was the answer. The idea of communicating directly with him had filled me with feelings of guilt and condemnation for my inadequacy before. Now I knew that he is pure, but he is also Love. He accepts me as I am and is helping me become the person his Spirit is prompting me to be. I was walking through my days with a Friend who was a Superior, but who accepted me.

Because I was loved and accepted, I could love back through worship. As I expressed praise, thankfulness, and joy in the Spirit, the bright side of my emotional nature began to emerge. Because of spiritual union, I could show my fears to God as I experienced them. In him I began to feel secure instead of afraid, confident instead of uncertain, capable instead of incapable, and peaceful instead of unsettled. A healthy emotional nature came from living at home in Jesus Christ in my spiritual woman.

CHOOSING WISELY

The ability to choose wisely is developed in the same fashion—by living at home in Jesus Christ. But it is one of the most difficult human challenges. Options are more varied than ever and we waver, fearing we'll make a mistake. Finally, we charge ahead desperately because we must do something.

Images of determined-looking women in dark suits and white blouses with brief cases in hand can be intimidating. *They don't flounder over whether to have pizza or hamburger for dinner. Why am I so inept?*

Many of us are learning to choose. *God, I'll do the best I can based on what I know.* Every small choice is a step toward a more disciplined will. Even the most insignificant is important. *I will put off the vacuuming until tomorrow and have coffee with my husband in front of the fireplace this evening.*

A choice Delores made when her children were small changed her life dramatically. "My husband's work took him away a lot, and I felt as though I was just hanging on. But through an act of my will, I decided that I'd be the best mother I could. I chose to spend time with my children, feeling grass on our feet, playing favorite records and lying on the rug to listen. At bedtime, I'd sit outside my daughter's room and listen to her tell stories to get herself to sleep. These were my sanity spots.

"The ability to make those choices came from God. I cried out to him all the time. Those years have tears all over them. I got my fulfillment in doing what was in front of me. Those years were my birthing seat, the decrusting of a twenty-one-year-old woman.'"

SPIRIT-CONTROLLED NONCONFORMITY

The woman who is a branch can learn to feel beautiful because the Beautiful One is united with her spirit. It is true that she can become more attractive by wearing flared skirts instead of gathered ones and tailored clothes instead of ruffles. But to count on Estee Lauder and Calvin Klein to dispel uncertainty about ourselves is to delay our progress to wholeness. Lasting confidence in our attractiveness even when we have zits or wrinkles comes when we honor the biblical order: value yourself because you are God's cherished daughter, home of his Spirit. Allow that to motivate you to make the best outward appearance that you can. Our unique reflection of the image of God is our greatest attribute. Love, packaged in our individuality and worn daily instead of kept for company best, is our greatest asset.

That individuality, expressed through our natural qualities, causes us to choose dramatic clothes over traditional ones and to cry at film scenes when the rest of the family is dry-eyed. In the past, I failed to understand that God meant me to remain me. So I sucked myself in here and chipped away at me there, trying to make myself honey-sweet and docile, the temperament I imagined was the only acceptable one for a Christian female. And I hated myself because I failed.

What I came to see is that Christ means for us to express his nature through Spirit-controlled nonconformity. The combination of our positive qualities—a Bombeckian sense of humor, sensitivity, optimism, gregariousness, quiet contemplativeness—is what makes us individual expressions of the nature of God. As we live at home in Christ, our positive qualities surface and he refines them. Our natural strengths are expressed more and our weaknesses less because we are under the Holy Spirit's control.

Journal Exercise: Begin cultivating your potential in each of the following ways:

1. No matter how you feel, first thing every morning sing a hymn of praise to God. Read aloud a Psalm of praise, such as 66; 93; 95:1-7; 98; 100; 136:1-9. Insert personal pronouns, such as "I give thanks to you Lord for you are good. Your love endures forever."

2. Cultivate your will by committing yourself to the Vine and letting him help you make a series of small daily choices, particularly ones that your old self objects to, like calling a new acquaintance if you're shy. Choosing correctly gradually comes easier. Write about what happens.

3. Decide what changes you can make in your appearance that show your growing sense of inner beauty and self-acceptance.

USING THE GIFTS GOD HAS GIVEN

The more we comprehend that this particular woman was chosen by God to be his very own even before he made the world and that she stands before him covered with his love (Ephesians 1:4), the more able we'll be to believe that he's gifted us with special abilities.

Before I saw myself as an Ephesians woman, I found it hard to believe that God had gifted me. The Bible said so. But like "God so loved the world," it was dogma to be underlined and outlined and taught in the assembly and embraced by my intellect. I worked, all right. But I worked indiscriminately, at anything ministry-related, whether I had the ability or not. Work gave me significance. Besides, I supposed that God or one of his executive vice-presidents in charge of the church expected me to, and I had to do what was expected.

After God's love settled in, my desire to discover my talents intensified. Can I become a writer? Could I be successful at it? After studying for months, I went to the public library to produce my first article. The editor to whom I sent it complimented me on what I'd written and promised to publish it. For my second article, I was paid.

I did have special abilities. Mine were to communicate through teaching (which I'd done already), and writing. I didn't have to do everything. I did have to use the gifts God had given me for the common good. As I matured, I discovered other abilities as well.

Annette was in her mid-thirties when her personal identity began to emerge. "My husband gets credit for the process. He kept telling me to relax and be myself. Not to be afraid to say 'No.'

"I outlined on paper what I thought were my strong points. I could see that they needed strengthening. And I saw that I had ministries in my weak areas. I was trying to be what someone else wanted me to be."

After her children were older, Evelyn began searching to discover her particular abilities. "I asked myself if I could do anything I wanted, what would it be? I came up with three things, and went down the list, investigating them to see if they were for me and eliminating them when I discovered they were not. When I got to writing, that's when I felt like I was who I was."

Even though we're too busy to devote hours a day to cultivating and exercising our talents, we can still begin. Ask God to show you what your abilities are. In answer, he'll unearth latent desires and give opportunities to begin cultivating them one by one.

Finally, he'll give opportunities to exercise them. We may not be able to write a book yet, but we can write articles for our church newsletter. We don't have time to be youth leader now, but we can be attending seminars to learn how, and establishing relationships with teens.

When Claire's children were small, she discovered a class on drawing on TV. "That became my program, and I began to learn to sketch. I really enjoyed it. Later, people in church heard about my drawing ability and asked me to work in the audio-visual department where it could be used."

THE FEAR OF FAILURE

Women's Ministry Director Reubena Poole said, "Many women are so afraid of failing that they don't try." In the search for her own talents, my friend Evelyn said, "The big thing for me was getting the whole failure idea out of the picture. I had to ask myself, 'What things would I do if I knew I wouldn't fail?'"

Annette remembers, "If I failed, I'd think, 'You don't deserve to live.' But then I watched to see how others handled failure. My husband was my most important teacher. He did the best he could, and if he didn't do a super job at something, it didn't bother him. I realized that I didn't have to do things perfectly, either. I began to learn to adopt the qualities I admired in others."

Journal Exercise: What are your special abilities? Do you feel as though you are bragging to mention them? Read 1 Corinthians 12:7. Ask yourself: Am I ministering in the area of my special abilities? What problems am I having? Discuss them with a close Christian friend.

If you haven't discovered your cluster of talents, work through the following steps:

1. Pray for God to help you discover one of your talents.

2. Learn how to use it.

3. Look for opportunities to use it. Take them.

4. Look for God's confirmation through the Spirit and other people.

5. When you are ready, ask God to help you discover another of your abilities and repeat the process.

MEET THE WOMAN WHO CAN

The more we use our abilities, the more others will tell us "Your song blessed me." "I love the way you arranged the church nursery. It's so much more attractive for the children and makes mothers feel better about leaving their babies."

Whether we're artists painting tumult ruled by Order or a math student keeping books for one of Christ's local assemblies, serving will be among the most fulfilling parts of our lives.

That's because we no longer have to prove our value by what we do. Our worth, we know, is measured by who we are. We are not significant because we make cakes from scratch instead of Pillsbury or design clothes for a living instead of slopping hogs. Our self is secure because she lives safely at home in Jesus Christ where she is loved and accepted.

With our egos safe in God's hands, we're free to become servants. Life gives us plenty of opportunities.

Your scenario may be a traffic jam or a long line at a supermarket. Or maybe you're up to your elbows in greasy water when your two-year-old toddles into the room and stands, legs apart, wet pants sagging, and looks at you. "Potty!" he says urgently. Your husband yells from the garage. "Bring the wrench that's on the table. And bring it now!"

You hurry to the garage with the wrench in your wet, greasy hand, then rush upstairs to change the baby's pants, catching the phone on the way. Your boss wants you to be at work an hour early in the morning and as you agree you wonder what you'll do about the sitter.

You want to scream at the baby, snap at your husband and slam down the phone. Instead, the woman within flashes a glance to the Vine, drops her anger in his lap and does what branches do best—she bears fruit.

1. *Webster's New World Dictionary of the American Languange.*
2. Kenneth S. Wuest, *Word Studies in the Greek New Testament,* vol. 1, (Grand Rapids: Wm. B. Eerdmans Publishing Co., 1973), p.88.

SCRIPTURE THAT TELLS OF GOD'S LOVE FOR YOU

Psalm 139
John 3:16 and 17
John 10:11-16
John 13:1-5
John 14:18-23
John 15:9; 10; 13
John 16:27
Romans 5:1-6
Romans 8:31-39
Ephesians 1:1-14
Ephesians 2:4-7
Ephesians 3:14-21
Ephesians 5:1 and 2

SCRIPTURE
THAT
DESCRIBES
GOD'S NATURE

Exodus 3:14
Job 38-39
Psalm 86:5 and 15
Psalm 89:1, 2, and 14
Psalm 136:1-9
Psalm 145:8, 9:17-19
1 Peter 1:16
2 Peter 3:9
Hebrews 6:10
Hebrews 12:5 and 6
Revelation 1:8

ADDITIONAL JOURNAL EXERCISES

CHAPTER ONE

1. What positive and negative qualities of your mother (or mother figures) shaped your idea of what a woman should be?
2. When you were growing up, what did you want to achieve in order to be successful? How has that changed over the years? Why? What is success to you now?
3. At what times do you feel as though you have no identity of your own? How do you respond to the feeling?

CHAPTER TWO

1. Imagine that you are a baby and Jesus is standing by your crib telling you about yourself. What things do you imagine he is saying?
2. Look for times you compare yourself to others and conclude that you are of lesser or greater worth than they. Why did you draw these conclusions and why are they inaccurate?
3. Write down times when TV, radio, and print media paint a false picture of what a successful person is. Why is it inaccurate? How have these ideas been influencing you?

CHAPTER THREE

1. Write a paragraph describing three ways in which you are God's own image. Write a second paragraph telling how that makes you feel about yourself.
2. Have you ever felt like an inferior human being because you are a woman? Find Scripture that proves this wrong.
3. What combination of characteristics makes you unique? Include nationality, physical and personality traits, intellectual ability, emotional make up. These are a gift from God to give you individuality. Why is this a most important gift?

CHAPTER FOUR

1. From the following passages, write as much as you can about the human spirit. Romans 8:16; 1 Corinthians 16:17 and 18; Luke 1:47; John 4:23 and 24.
2. What do they show you about your spirit?

CHAPTER FIVE

1. Have you disbelieved in the depth and consistency of God's love? Taken it for granted? Seen his love as less real than human love? Have you believed he loves

you only on certain occasions? Record your thoughts and conclusions.

2. Has your relationship with a parent colored the way you see God? How?

3. Look up three names by which Jesus is called. How do they reveal God's love?

4. Reflect on the lives of biblical characters with whom God dealt lovingly in spite of their inconsistencies. Remember that he has the same attitude toward you. Respond to him about that.

CHAPTER SIX

1. Paste a snapshot of yourself in your journal. Begin to look at that person as someone whom God loves. What is there about you that makes him love you? About him? Write a letter to yourself telling why he loves you.

2. Write out a definition of grace that is different from the one you've known. In the following Scriptures, how does God's grace demonstrate his love? 2 Corinthians 12:9; 1 Timothy 1:12-14; Ephesians 2:4-7.

3. Meditate on the verses of "Amazing Grace." Sing or say the words to God. Which parts mean the most and why?

CHAPTER SEVEN

1. Study 1 John 3:1 in the NIV. "How great is the love the Father has lavished on us, that we should be called children of God! And that is what we are!" When is the last time someone lavished love on you? How did you feel? Think of five ways God has lavished love on you.

2. Describe one material possession you cherish above all others. Why? How do you care for it? Use it as an illustration of God's love and care of you.

3. Record the formula for change in your journal. Which parts are hardest for you? Think of two things

you can do to improve. Begin to do them and record what happens.

CHAPTER EIGHT

1. Choose a fruitbearing tree or plant near your home as a picture of John 10. How many ways are you alike and different? Let God use it as an illustration of abiding when you pass it. Write what he shows you.
2. Have you been confused about what it means to bear fruit? How? What insight do you receive from Psalm 1:2 and 3; Romans 5:3; 2 Peter 1:3-9?
3. Write a paragraph telling what abiding in Christ means to you.

CHAPTER NINE

1. Explain the difference between giving yourself away and giving out from yourself. Which is the biblical way? Why? What things do you need to do to live that way?
2. Are you making impossible demands on yourself? Allowing others to do so? Why? Pinpoint the most trying time in your day and think of a way to change it.
3. Which of the following would make you a more effective branch? A more healthful diet? More sleep? Regular exercise? Make yourself accountable to another Christian to change in this area and write your experiences.

CHAPTER TEN

1. Jesus was a carpenter and a preacher. Did he use these roles to give him identity or did he describe who he was some other way? What did he say? How does that relate to you?
2. Every day that you have the opportunity, find one way to relate to another woman whom you do not know. Perhaps it will be just a smile or a word of casual conversation. Cultivate this as a practice and

write about their responses and your own.

3. What one person has been hard to get along with because they have been unkind to you? Have you been expecting them to give love of which they're incapable? Meditate on 1 John 4:11 and think of ways you can change your attitude toward them even if they don't change their attitude toward you.

CHAPTER ELEVEN

1. Think of one Christian you know who went through a crisis and maintained their faith. Ask them to tell you how they did it. Write what you learn.

2. Write Hebrews 12:12 and 13 in your own words. Put your own name in at the beginning of verse 12. What lame place in your personality do you want God to heal?

3. There are six potential crises mentioned in Habakkuk 3:17 and 18. Insert six potential crises that you could face, such as "Though I lose my job." How many have you faced already? What have you learned? Make a personal commitment to God to go to him for abiding faith at such times.

CHAPTER TWELVE

1. Each of the following Scriptures shows a way a Christian can grow strong. Choose one and find out all you can about the principle involved. Be sure to define key words. How can you apply the principle? Begin to do so and record your experiences. Then go on to another verse: Proverbs 24:5; Romans 4:20 and 21; 2 Corinthians 12:7-10; 2 Timothy 2:1.

2. Has an unbiblical self-concept kept you from cultivating your potential? Why and how? What steps can you take to change that? Act on what you see.

3. Read a book on a subject you've always wanted to learn more about. Draw personal conclusions and write them.

4. Which of your personal traits do you mourn most? Ask God to enable you to replace it with its opposite. Accept situations he brings to help you learn to do that. Write ways God answers your prayer and thank him.
5. Go back to any journal exercises in this book that need more work.
6. Continue writing your growing experiences as you learn to live at home in Jesus Christ.

The author is available for seminars. For information, contact Multnomah Press, 10209 S.E. Division, Portland, Oregon 97266.